ASSYRIAN HISTORIOGRAPHY
A SOURCE STUDY

THE
UNIVERSITY OF MISSOURI STUDIES

SOCIAL SCIENCE SERIES
Volume III   Number 1

ASSYRIAN HISTORIOGRAPHY

A Source Study

By
ALBERT TEN EYCK OLMSTEAD
Associate Professor of Ancient History

WIPF & STOCK · Eugene, Oregon

Wipf and Stock Publishers
199 W 8th Ave, Suite 3
Eugene, OR 97401

Assyrian Historiography
A Source Study
By Olsmstead, Albert Ten Eyck
ISBN 13: 978-1-60608-303-1
Publication date 11/21/2008
Previously published by University of Missouri, 1916

CONTENTS

CHAPTER I
Assyrian Historians and their Histories.................... 1

CHAPTER II
The Beginnings of True History
 (Tiglath Pileser I)................................10

CHAPTER III
The Development of Historical Writing
 (Ashur nasir apal and Shalmaneser III)...............15

CHAPTER IV
Shamshi Adad and the Synchronistic History...............29

CHAPTER V
Sargon and the Modern Historical Criticism................36

CHAPTER VI
Annals and Display Inscriptions
 (Sennacherib and Esarhaddon).......................43

CHAPTER VII
Ashur bani apal and Assyrian Editing.....................53

CHAPTER VIII
The Babylonian Chronicle and Berossus...................59

CHAPTER I

ASSYRIAN HISTORIANS AND THEIR HISTORIES

To the serious student of Assyrian history, it is obvious that we cannot write that history until we have adequately discussed the sources. We must learn what these are, in other words, we must begin with a bibliography of the various documents. Then we must divide them into their various classes, for different classes of inscriptions are of varying degrees of accuracy. Finally, we must study in detail for each reign the sources, discover which of the various documents or groups of documents are the most nearly contemporaneous with the events they narrate, and on these, and on these alone, base our history of the period.

To the less narrowly technical reader, the development of the historical sense in one of the earlier culture peoples has an interest all its own. The historical writings of the Assyrians form one of the most important branches of their literature. Indeed, it may be claimed with much truth that it is the most characteristically Assyrian of them all.[1]

---

[1] This study is a source investigation and not a bibliography. The only royal inscriptions studied in detail are those presenting source problems. Minor inscriptions of these rulers are accorded no more space than is absolutely necessary, and rulers who have not given us strictly historical inscriptions are generally passed in silence. The bibliographical notes are condensed as much as possible and make no pretense of completeness, though they will probably be found the most complete yet printed. Every possible care has been taken to make the references accurate, but the fact that many were consulted in the libraries of Cornell University, University of Chicago, Columbia University, and the University of Pennsylvania, and are thus inaccessible at the time when the work is passing through the press, leaves some possibility of error. Dr. B. B. Charles, Instructor in

The Assyrians derived their historical writing, as they did so many other cultural elements, from the Babylonians. In that country, there had existed from the earliest times two types of historical inscriptions. The more common form developed from the desire of the kings to commemorate, not their deeds in war, but their building operations, and more especially the buildings erected in honor of the gods. Now and then we have an incidental reference to military activities, but rarely indeed do we find a document devoted primarily to the narration of warlike deeds. Side by side with these building inscriptions were to be found dry lists of kings, sometimes with the length of their reigns, but, save for an occasional legend, there seem to have been no detailed histories. It was from the former type that the earliest Assyrian inscriptions were derived. In actual fact, we have no right to call them historical in any sense of the word, even though they are our only sources for the few facts we know about this early period. A typical inscription of this type will have the form "Irishum the vice gerent of the god Ashur, the son of Ilushuma the vice gerent of the god Ashur, unto the god Ashur, his Lord, for his own life and for the life of his son has dedicated". Thus there was as yet little difference in form from their Babylonian models and the historical data were of the slightest. This type persisted until the latest days of the Assyrian empire in the inscriptions placed on the bricks, or, in slightly more developed form, in the inscriptions written on the slabs of stone used for the adornment of palace or temple. For these later periods, they rarely have a value other than for the

Semitics in the University of Pennsylvania, has kindly verified those where error has seemed at all likely.—For the English speaking reader, practically all the inscriptions for the earlier half of the history are found in Budge-King, *Annals of the Kings of Assyria. 1.* For the remainder, Harper, *Assyrian and Babylonian Literature*, is adequate, though somewhat out of date. Rogers, *Cuneiform Parallels to the Old Testament*, gives an up to date translation of those passages which throw light on the Biblical writings. Other works cited are generally of interest only to specialists and the most common are cited by abbreviations which will be found at the close of the study.

architectural history, and so demand no further study in this place. Nevertheless, the architectural origin of the historical inscription should not be forgotten. Even to the end, it is a rare document which does not have as its conclusion a more or less full account of the building operations carried on by the monarch who erected it.

It was not long until the inscriptions were incised on limestone. These slabs, giving more surface for the writing, easily induced the addition of other data, including naturally some account of the monarch's exploits in war. The typical inscription of this type, take, for example that of Adad nirari I,[1] has a brief titulary, then a slightly longer sketch of the campaigns, but the greater portion by far is devoted to the narration of his buildings. This type also continued until the latest days of the empire, and, like the former, is of no value where we have the fuller documents.

When the German excavations were begun at Ashur, the earliest capital of the Assyrian empire, it was hoped that the scanty data with which we were forced to content ourselves in writing the early history would soon be much amplified. In part, our expectations have been gratified. We now know the names of many new rulers and the number of new inscriptions has been enormously increased. But not a single annals inscription from this earlier period has been discovered, and it is now becoming clear that such documents are not to be expected. Only the so-called "Display" inscriptions, and those with the scantiest content, have been found, and it is not probable that any will be hereafter discovered.

It was not until the end of the fourteenth century B. C., with the reign of Arik den ilu, that we have the appearance of actual annalistic inscriptions. That we are at the very begin-

[1]BM. 90,978; IV. R. 44f.; G. Smith, *Assyr. Discoveries*, 1875, 242ff.; Pognon, JA. 1884, 293ff. Peiser, KB. I. 4ff.; Budge-King, 4ff.; duplicate Scheil, RT. XV. 138ff.; Jastrow, ZA. X. 35ff; AJSL. XII. 143ff.

ning of annalistic writing is clear, even from the fragmentary remains. The work is in annals form, in so far as the events of the various years are separated by lines, but it is hardly more than a list of places captured and of booty taken, strung together by a few formulae.[1]

With this one exception, we do not have a strictly historical document nor do we have any source problem worthy of our study until the time of Tiglath Pileser I, about 1100 B. C. To be sure, we have a good plenty of inscriptions before this time,[2] and the problems they present are serious enough, but they are not of the sort that can be solved by source study. Accordingly, we shall begin our detailed study with the inscriptions from this reign. Then, after a gap in our knowledge, caused by the temporary decline of Assyrian power, we shall take up the many problems presented by the numerous inscriptions of Ashur nasir apal (885-860 B. C.) and of his son Shalmaneser III (860-825 B. C.). In the case of the latter, especially, we shall see how a proper evaluation of the documents secures a proper appreciation of the events in the reign. With these we shall discuss their less important successors until the downfall of the dynasty. The revival of Assyrian power under Tiglath Pileser IV (745-728 B. C.) means a revival of history writing and our problems begin again. The Sargonidae, the most important of the various Assyrian dynasties, comprising Sargon (722-705 B. C.), Sennacherib (705-686 B. C.), Esarhaddon (686-668 B. C.), and Ashur bani apal (668-626 B. C.), furnish us a most embarassing wealth of historical material, while the problems, especially as to priority of date and as to consequent authority, become most complicated.

Before taking up a more detailed study of these questions, it is necessary to secure a general view of the situation we must

[1] Scheil, OLZ. VII. 216. Now in the Morgan collection, Johns, *Cuneiform Inscriptions*, 33.

[2] L. Messerschmidt, *Keilschrifttexte aus Assur*. I. Berlin 1911; *Mittheilungen der Deutschen Orient Gesellschaft;* cf. D. D. Luckenbill, AJSL. XXVIII. 153ff.

face. The types of inscriptions, especially in the later days of the empire, are numerous. In addition to the brick and slab inscriptions, rarely of value in this later period, we have numerous examples on a larger scale of the so called "Display" inscriptions. They are usually on slabs of stone and are intended for architectural adornment. In some cases, we have clay tablets with the original drafts prepared for the workmen. Still others are on clay prisms or cylinders. These latter do not differ in form from many actual annals, but this likeness in form should not blind us to the fact that their text is radically different in character.

All the display inscriptions are primarily of architectural character, whether intended to face the walls of the palace or to be deposited as a sort of corner stone under the gates or at the corners of the wall. We should not expect their value to be high, and indeed they are of but little worth when the corresponding annals on which they are based has been preserved. For example, we have four different recensions of a very long display inscription, as well as literally scores of minor ones, also of a display character, from the later years of Sargon. The minor inscriptions are merely more or less full abstracts of the greater and offer absolutely nothing new. The long display inscription might be equally well disregarded, had not the edition of the annals on which it is based come down to us in fragmentary condition. We may thus use the Display inscription to fill gaps in the Annals, but it has not the slightest authority when it disagrees with its original.

It is true that for many reigns, even at a fairly late date, the display inscriptions are of great value. For the very important reign of Adad nirari (812-785 B. C.), it is our only recourse as the annals which we may postulate for such a period of development are totally lost. The deliberate destruction of the greater portion of the annals of Tiglath Pileser IV forces us to study the display documents in greater detail and the loss of all but a fragment of the annals of Esarhaddon makes for this period, too, a fuller discussion of the display inscriptions than would be otherwise necessary. In addition, we may note that there are a few inscriptions from other reigns, for example, the Nimrud inscription of Sargon, which are seemingly based on an earlier edition of the annals than that which has come down to us and which therefore do give us a few new facts.

Since, then, it is necessary at times to use these display inscriptions, we must frankly recognize their inferior value. We must realize that their main purpose was not to give a connected history of the reign, but simply to list the various conquests for the greater glory of the monarch. Equally serious is it that they rarely have a chronological order. Instead, the survey generally follows a geographical sweep from east to west. That they are to be used with caution is obvious.

Much more fortunate is our position when we have to deal with the annalistic inscriptions. We have here a regular chronology, and if errors, intentional or otherwise, can sometimes be found, the relative chronology at least is generally correct. The narrative is fuller and interesting details not found in other sources are often given. But it would be a great mistake to assume that the annals are always trustworthy. Earlier historians have too generally accepted their statements unless they had definite proof of inaccuracy. In the last few years, there has been discovered a mass of new material which we may use for the criticism of the Sargonide documents. Most valuable are the letters, sometimes from the king himself, more often from others to the monarch. Some are from the generals in the field, others from the governors in the provinces, still others from palace officials. All are of course absolutely authentic documents, and the light they throw upon the annals is interesting. To these we may add the prayers at the oracle of the sun god, coming from the reigns of Esarhaddon and Ashur bani apal, and they show us the break up of the empire as we never should have suspected from the grandiloquent accounts of the monarchs themselves. Even the business documents occasionally yield us a slight help toward criticism. Add to this the references in foreign sources such as Hebrew or Babylonian, and we hardly need internal study to convince us that the annals are far from reliable.

Yet even internal evidence may be utilized. For example, when the king is said to have been the same year in two widely separated parts of the empire, warring with the natives, it is clear that in one of these the deeds of a general have been falsely ascribed to the king, and the suspicion is raised that he may have been at home in Assyria all the time. That there are many such false attributions to the king is proved by much other evidence, the letters from the generals in command to their ruler; an occasional reference to outside authorities, as when the editor of the book of Isaiah shows that the famous Ashdod expedition was actually led by the Turtanu or prime minister; or such a document as the dream of Ashur bani apal, which clearly shows that he was a frightened degenerate who had not the stamina to take his place in the field with the generals whose victories he usurped.

Again, various versions differ among themselves. To what a degree this is true, only those who have made a detailed study of the documents can appreciate. Typical examples from Sargon's Annals were pointed out several years ago.[1] The most striking of these, the murder of the Armenian king Rusash by — the cold blooded Assyrian scribe,— has now been clearly proved false by a contemporaneous document emanating from Sargon himself. Another good illustration is found in the cool taking by Ashur bani apal of bit after bit of the last two Egyptian campaigns of his father until in the final edition there is nothing that he has not claimed for himself.

The Assyrians, as their business documents show, could be exceedingly exact with numbers. But this exactness did not extend to their historical inscriptions. We could forgive them for giving us in round numbers the total of enemies slain or of booty carried off and even a slight exaggeration would be pardonable. But what shall we say as to the accuracy of numbers in our documents when one edition gives the total slain in a battle as 14,000, another as 20,500, the next as 25,000, and the last as 29,000! Is it surprising that we begin to wonder whether the

[1] Olmstead, *Western Asia in the Reign of Sargon of Assyria*, 1908.

victory was only a victory on the clay tablet of the scribe? What shall we say when we find that the reviser has transformed a booty of 1,235 sheep in his original into a booty of 100,225! This last procedure, the addition of a huge round number to the fairly small amount of the original, is a common trick of the Sargonide scribe, of which many examples may be detected by a comparison of Sargon's Display inscription with its original, the Annals. So when Sennacherib tells us that he took from little Judah no less than 200,150 prisoners, and that in spite of the fact that Jerusalem itself was not captured, we may deduct the 200,000 as a product of the exuberant fancy of the Assyrian scribe and accept the 150 as somewhere near the actual number captured and carried off.

This discussion has led to another problem, that of the relative order of the various annals editions. For that there were such various editions can be proved for nearly every reign. And in nearly every reign it has been the latest and worst edition which has regularly been taken by the modern historians as the basis for their studies. How prejudicial this may be to a correct view of the Assyrian history, the following pages will show. The procedure of the Assyrian scribe is regularly the same. As soon as the king had won his first important victory, the first edition of the annals was issued. With the next great victory, a new edition was made out. For the part covered by the earlier edition, an abbreviated form of this was incorporated. When the scribe reached the period not covered by the earlier document, he naturally wrote more fully, as it was more vividly in his mind and therefore seemed to him to have a greater importance. Now it would seem that all Assyriologists should have long ago recognized that *any one of these editions is of value only when it is the most nearly contemporaneous of all those preserved. When it is not so contemporaneous, it has absolutely no value when we do have the original from which it was derived.* Yet it still remains true that the most accessible editions of these annals are those which are the latest and poorest. Many of the earlier and more valuable editions have not been republished for many years, so that for our most contemporaneous sources we must often go to old books, long out of print and difficult to secure, while both translation and commentary are hopelessly behind the times. Particularly is this the case with the inscriptions of Sennacherib and Ashur bani apal. The greatest boon to the historian of Assyria would be an edition of the Assyrian historical inscriptions in which would be given only those editions or portions of editions which may be considered as contemporaneous and of first class value. With such a collection before him, notable as much for what it excluded as for what was included, many of the most stubborn problems in Assyrian history would cease to be problems.

The historian of Assyria must test his sources before he can use them in his history. To do this, he must first of all be able to distinguish the primary sources which will reward future study from those which are secondary and are based on other and more contemporary documents which even now are actually in our possession. When these latter are cast aside as of no practical value, save perhaps as they show the peculiar mental operations of the Assyrian editor, we are then ready to test the remainder by the various methods known to the historian. The second part of this task must be worked out by the historian when he studies the actual history in detail. It is the discovery of what are the primary sources for the various reigns and of the value of the contributions which they make to Assyrian history that is to be the subject of the more detailed discussion in the following chapters.

CHAPTER II

THE BEGINNINGS OF TRUE HISTORY

(Tiglath Pileser I)

We shall begin, then, our detailed study of the sources for Assyrian history with the data for the reign of Tiglath Pileser I. (circa 1100 B. C.). Taking up first the Annals, we find that the annalistic documents from the reign may be divided into two general groups. One, the Annals proper, is the so called Cylinder, in reality written on a number of hexagonal prisms.[1] First comes the praise of the gods and self praise of the ruler himself. Then follow the campaigns, not numbered as in the more developed style of later rulers, but separated into six sections, for the six years whose events are narrated, by brief glorifications of the monarch. Next we have the various hunting exploits of the king, and the document ends with an elaborate account of the building operations and with threats against the later ruler who should destroy the inscription or refuse credit to the king in whose honor it was made.

No relationship has been made out between the fragments, but the four fairly complete prisms fall into two groups, A and C, B and D, as regards both the form of writing and the char-

---

[1]Photographs of B and A, Budge-King, xliii; xlvii; of the Ashur fragments, of at least five prisms, Andrä, *Anu-Adad Tempel*, Pl. xiii. ff. I R. 9ff.; Winckler, *Sammlung*, I. 1ff.; Budge-King, 27ff., with variants and BM numbers. Lotz, *Inschriften Tiglathpilesers* I, 1880; Winckler, KB. I. 14ff. Rawlinson, Hincks, Talbot, Oppert, JRAS. OS. XVIII. 150ff.; Oppert, *Histoire des empires de Chaldée et d'Assyrie*, 1865, 44f.; Menant, 35ff.; Rawlinson, RP¹, V. 7ff.; Sayce RP², I. 92ff.; Muss-Arnolt in Harper, 11ff.; MDOG. 25, 21f.; 28, 22; 29, 40; 47, 33; King, *Supplement*, 116; Andrä, *Tempel*, 32ff.

ASSYRIAN HISTORIOGRAPHY 11

acter of the text. All date seemingly from the same month of the same year, though from separate days. The most fragmentary of these, D, seems the best, as it has the smallest number of unique readings and has also the largest number of omissions,[1] all of which are clearly interpolations in the places where they are given. This is especially true of the one[2] which refers to the Anu-Adad and Ishtar temples, for not only is the insertion awkward, we know from the Obelisk[3] that the Anu-Adad temple was not completed till year five, so that it must be an interpolation of that date. In spite of its general resemblance to D, especially in its omissions, B is very poorly written and has over two hundred unique readings. One of its omissions would seriously disarrange the chronology,[4] others are clearly unwarranted,[5] and one long addition[6] further marks its peculiar character. Our conclusion must be that it is a poor copy of a good original. C is between A and B, agreeing with the latter in a strange interpolation[7] and in the omission of the five kings of the Muski.[8] A is the latest but best preserved, while the character of the text warrants us in making this our standard as it has but few unique readings and but one improbable omission.[9] The same account, in slightly different form and seemingly later in date[10] is also found in some tablet inscriptions.[11]

[1] II. 21b-23a; III. 37b-39a; IV. 36.
[2] IV. 36.
[3] II. 13.
[4] IV. 40-42.
[5] II. 79-81; V. 4; VIII. 29b-33.
[6] VII. 17-27; also I. 35; different in VI. 37.
[7] III. 2a-c.
[8] I. 63b. King, *Supplement*, 116 follows C.
[9] VII. 105-8.
[10] K. 2815 is dated in the eponomy of Ninib nadin apal, the LAH MA GAL E official. He probably is after the rab bi lul official in whose year the hexagons are dated.
[11] Budge-King, 125 n.3; K.2815, with different conclusion; 81-2-4, 220, where reverse different; K.12009; K.13840; 79-7-8, 280; 89-4-26, 28; Rm. 573; Winckler, AOF. III. 245.

A second annalistic group is that postulated as the original of the so called Broken Obelisk. Of documents coming directly from Tiglath Pileser himself, the only one that can with any probability be assigned to this is the tiny fragment which refers to the capture of Babylon.[1] But that such a group did exist is proved by the extracts from it in the obelisk prepared by a descendant of Tiglath Pileser, probably one of his sons, Shamshi Adad or Ashur bel kala.[2] Only the upper portion, probably less than half to judge by the proportions, is preserved, and even this is terribly mutilated. Fortunately, the parts best preserved are those relating to the years not dealt with in the Annals. The first half of the document is devoted to the campaigns of Tiglath Pileser, then come his hunting exploits, and only a bit at the end is reserved for the building operations of the unknown ruler under whom it was erected. Its source seems to have had the same relation to the earliest form of the Annals that the Obelisk of Shalmaneser III had to the Monolith, that is, it gave the data for the earlier part of the reign, that covered by the other source, very briefly, only expanding as it reached a period where the facts were not represented by any other document. That our earlier Annals, or perhaps rather, one of its sources, was a main source of our second type, is proved by the coincidences in language in the two, in one case no less than twenty signs the same,[3] not to speak of the hunting expeditions. But this earlier Annals was not the only, or at least not the direct source for the Obelisk, nor was that source merely a fuller recension of it. Data for the first six years, not found in the earlier Annals, are

[1] K. 10042; Winckler, AOF. I. 387.
[2] Photograph, Budge-King, li; Paterson, *Assyr. Sculptures*, 63. I R. 28; III R. 4, 1; Budge-King, 128ff. Lotz, *op. cit.*, 196ff.; Peiser, KB. I. 122ff.; Talbot, JRAS. OS. XIX. 124ff.; Houghton-Finlay, RP¹, XI. 9ff.; Oppert, *Hist.*, 132ff.; Hommel, *Gesch.*, 532ff.; Menant, 49ff. Proved to Tiglath Pileser, Lotz, *op. cit.*, 193f.; cf. Budge-King, 131 n. 4, though Streck, ZA. XVIII. 187ff., still believes that it belongs to an earlier king. Found at Nineveh, though it deals with Ashur constructions.
[3] In year V we have *ishtu...adi alu Kargamish sha matu Hatte...isu elippe pl mashku tahshe.*

given in the Obelisk,[1] while our document also, for the first time in Assyrian historical inscriptions, dates the events by the name of the eponym for the year, and, still more unusual, by the month as well. That the Obelisk may be considered merely a resume of this original source is shown by the statement that he conquered other lands and made many wars, but these he did not record.[2] As they seem to have been given after the hunting feats, in the lost lower part of column IV, we may assume that all that preceded is taken from that source. Furthermore, we are given the other hunting exploits "which my [father] did not record."[3] The numbers of beasts killed, which the scribe intended especially to emphasize, have never, curiously enough, been inscribed in the blanks left for their insertion.[4]

Opposed to the Annals proper are the Display inscriptions in which chronological considerations and details as to the campaigns are subordinated to the desire to give a general view of the monarch's might. Two have been found in foreign lands, one at the source of the Tigris,[5] the other near Melazgerd in Armenia.[6] Drafts for similar inscriptions have been found on clay tablets, written for the use of the workmen who were to incise

[1] Obl. I. 17, reference to Marduk nadin ahe, King of Akkad; II. 1, one thousand men of land of...; II. 2, four thousand of them carried prisoner to Assyria, the position of which shows that it cannot, with Budge-King, 132 n., be referred to Ann. III. 2, the Kashi; II. 12, the Mushki (?); II. 13, temple of Anu and Adad. These all precede the Carchemish episode.

[2] Obl. IV. 37.

[3] Obl. IV. 33.

[4] E. g., Obl. IV. 4.

[5] Discovery, J. Taylor, cf. H. Rawlinson, *Athenaeum*, 1862, II. 811; 1863, I. 229. III R. 4, 6; Schrader, *Abh. K. Preuss. Akad.*, 1885, I. Winckler, *Sammlung*, I. 30: Budge-King, 127 n. 1. Meissner, *Chrestomathie*, 6; Abel-Winckler, 5; Menant, 49. Winckler, KB. I. 48f. Dated after the Arvad expedition as shown by reference to Great Sea of Amurru, and of same date as Melazgerd inscription, Belck, *Verh. Berl.*

[6] From Gonjalu, near Melazgerd, Belck-Lehmann, *Verh. Berl. Anthr. Ges.* 1898, 574. Photograph, Lehmann, *Sitzungsber. Berl. Akad.*, 1900, 627. Is this one of the "cuneiform inscriptions near Moosh" reported to Taylor, *Athenaeum*, 1863, I. 229?

them on stone. Of these, one, which is virtually complete as regards number of lines, seems to date from year four as it has no reference to later events.[1] It would then be our earliest extant source. It is also of value in dating the erection of the palace whose mention shows that the tablet is complete. That the compiler had before him the document used by the Annals in its account of the Nairi campaign[2] is proved by his writing "from Tumme to Daiene" for these are the first and last names in the well known list of Nairi states. The order of the tablet is neither chronological nor geographical. Another tablet dates from year five to which most of its data belong. In the first half, it follows the order of Tablet I, and in the remainder follows closely the words of its source in the Annals, merely abbreviating.[3] Possibly in its present form, it may be later than year five[4] for a third tablet of year ten duplicates this first part.[5] Unfortunately, this latter gives next to no historical data, but its reference to the "Lower Zab" and to the "Temple of Ishtar" may perhaps allow us to date to this same tenth year the highly important tablet which gives a full account of the campaign in Kirhi and Lulume and which also ends with the restoration of the Ishtar temple.[6] Here too and not with the Annals must be placed the fragment with the Arvad episode.[7]

[1] S. 1874; K. 2805, Tabl. I of Budge-King, 109ff. III R. 5; Winckler, *Sammlung*, I. 26ff.; cf. Lotz, *op. cit.*, 193; Tiele, Gesch., 159 n. 2; Meissner, ZA. IX. 101ff. Meissner's restoration of these as parts of one tablet in chronological order will not stand in view of the fact that I is complete in itself while there are variations in the order of Nairi and totally different endings.

[2] Ann. IV. 71ff.

[3] K. 2806 with K. 2804, Tabl. II of Budge-King, 116ff.

[4] The badly damaged reverse of K. 2806 has one reference to the Euphrates which *may* be connected with Obl. III. 24, probably of year IX.

[5] K. 2804, Tabl. V of Budge-King, 125f.

[6] K. 2807; 91-5-9, 196. III R. 5, 4; Tablet IV of Budge-King, 121ff. Winckler, AOF. III. 246. Hommel, *Gesch.*, 511f.

[7] Scheil, RT. XXII. 157. Restorations, Streck, ZA. XVIII. 186 n. 2. First attributed to Tiglath Pileser, Peiser, OLZ. III. 476; Winckler, ibid. IV. 296; cf. AOF. III. 247.—Bricks I R. 6, 5; Scheil, *op. cit.* 37; Winckler, *Sammlung*, I. 31; Budge-King, 127. Other inss., King, *Supplement*, 453, 488.

CHAPTER III

THE DEVELOPMENT OF HISTORICAL WRITING

(Ashur nasir apal and Shalmaneser III)

After the death of Tiglath Pileser, there is a period of darkness. A few bricks and other minor inscriptions give us the names of the rulers and possibly a bit of other information, but there is not a single inscription which is important enough to furnish source problems. It is not until we reach the reign of Tukulti Ninib (890-885) that we again have an Annals[1] and not until the reign of his son Ashur nasir apal (885-860) that we have problems of the sources.

The problem of the sources for the reign of Ashur nasir apal may be approached from a somewhat different angle than we took for those of Tiglath Pileser. Here we have a single document, the so called Annals, which gives practically all the known data of the reign. Earlier writers on the history of Assyria have therefore generally contented themselves with references to this one document, with, at most, an occasional reference to the others. This should not blind us, however, to the fact that the problem of the sources is by no means as simple as this. Indeed, for far the greater portion of the events given in the Annals, we have earlier and better sources. We may therefore best attack the problem as to the sources of the reign by working out the sources of the Annals.

Taking up the introduction to the Annals,[2] it at once strikes us as curious that it consists of a hymn to Ninib, at the entrance

---

[1]Scheil, *Annales de Tukulti Ninip* II, 1909; cf. Winckler, OLZ. XIII. 112ff.

[2]I R. 17ff.; Budge-King, 254ff.; Le Gac, *Les Inscriptions d'Assur-Nasir-Aplu* III. 1907, 1ff. Peiser, KB. I. 50ff.; H. Lhotzky, *Annalen*

to whose temple these slabs were placed, and not of a general invocation to the gods, beginning with Ashur, such as we are accustomed to find in other annalistic inscriptions. Further, we have other slabs in which this Ninib hymn occurs as a separate composition,[1] and this leads us to assume that it is not the original introduction. This is still further confirmed by the fact that we do find such a required invocation in the beginning of the Monolith inscription. Clearly, this is the original invocation. The second section of the Annals begins with the praise of the monarch, and here too begins the parallelism with the Monolith. The last events mentioned in the Monolith date from 880 and it is thus far earlier than our present edition of the Annals, which contains events from so late a date as 867. To this extent, then, the Monolith is a better document. It was not, however, the direct source of the Annals, as is shown by certain cases where the latter has preserved the better readings of proper names. Indeed, we should not over rate the Monolith, for it too is a compilation like its younger sister, and is by no means free from obvious mistakes, though in general better than the Annals.[2] For some portions of this earlier section, we have also separate slabs with small portions of the text,[3] and these regularly agree with the Monolith as against the Annals.[4]

Asurnazirpals, 1885. Oppert, *Expédition en Mésopotamie*, 1863, I. 311ff.; Rodwell, RP[1], III. 37ff.; Sayce, RP[2], II. 134ff.; Menant, 67ff.; *Manuel*, 1880, 335ff.

[1]Slabs 27-30, Budge-King, 255 n. — Other invocations are the Bel altar at Kalhu, BM. 71, Budge-King 160; Strong, JRAS. 1891, 157; and the Ishtar lion BM. 96, II R. 66, 1; S. A. Strong, RP[2], IV. 91f.; dupl. Budge-King, 206ff.

[2]BM. 847. Photograph, Budge-King, lxix; Paterson, *Assyr. Sculptures*, 64. I R. 27; Budge-King, 242ff.; cf. 254ff.; Le Gac, 129ff. Peiser, KB. I. 118ff. Menant, 66f.; Talbot, *Trans. Roy. Soc. Lit.*, VII. 189ff.; RP[1], VII. 15ff.

[3]BM. 90830, cf. Budge-King, 255 n.; L. 48f.

[4]I. 57, transposition; I. 69, the significant omission of *shadu;* and a large number of cases where they agree in spelling as against the Annals.

For the last of these years, 880, we have also the inscription from Kirkh,[1] which contains data for this year alone, and ends abruptly with the return from Nairi. This might be expected from its location at Tushhan, on the border of that country, and we are therefore warranted in assuming that it was set up here immediately after the return from the campaign and that in it we have a strictly contemporaneous document. Judged by this, the Annals, and even the Monolith, do not rank very high. Important sections are omitted by each, in fact, they seem to agree in these omissions, though in general they agree fairly closely with the account set up in the border city. It would seem as if the official narrative of the campaign had been prepared at Kirkh, immediately after its close, by the scribes who followed the army.[2] One copy of this became the basis of the Kirkh inscription while another was made at Kalhu and it was from this that the Monolith and Annals are derived.[3] From this, too, must have been derived the slab which gives a fourth witness for this section.[4]

With this year, 880, the Monolith fails us. But even if we had no other document, the Annals itself would show us that the year 880 was an important one in the development of our sources. At the end of the account for this year, we have a closing paragraph, taken bodily from the Ninib inscription, which may thus be assigned to 880. This is further confirmed by the manner in which this passage in the Annals abstracts the last lines of the Monolith,[5] which is repeated almost in its entirety at

[1] III R. 6; Budge-King, 222ff.; Le Gac, 137ff. Peiser, KB. I. 92ff.
[2] Cf. Johns, *Assyr. Deeds and Documents*, II. 168.
[3] Ann. II. 109, where Mon. has 300 as against 700 of Kir. and Ann., shows Ann. did not use Kir. through Mon.; Kir. has 40 as against 50 of the others in II. 111, and 200 for 2000 in II. 115; proper names such as Tushha for Tushhan show nearness of Mon. to Kir., but the likeness can hardly be considered striking.
[4] L. 48f.
[5] Ann. II. 125-135a is the same as the Ninib inscription 1-23a (BM. 30; Budge-King, 209ff.), and this in turn is merely a resume of the close of the Monolith.

the close of the Annals itself. The column thus ends a separate document, whose last line, giving a list of temples erected, seems to go back to one recension of the Standard inscription, which in its turn goes back to the various separate building inscriptions.

That the Annals itself existed in several recensions is indicated by the fact that, while there are no less than at least seventeen different duplicates of Column I,[1] there are but seven of II and five of III; that there is one of II only[2] and one of III;[3] and that there is still another, in at least three exemplars, in which parts of the Standard and Altar inscriptions are interpolated between the Ninib invocation and the main inscription.[4]

The year 880 marks also the removal of the capital from Nineveh to Kalhu,[5] which indicates that to this year we are to attribute the majority of the building inscriptions. But, as they are all more or less identical with the closing section of the Annals, we may best discuss them in that place. Continuing with the Annals, we now reach a section where it is the only source. And just here the Annals is lacking in its most essential feature, an exact chronology, no doubt because the dated year was not given in the source, though the months are carefully noted! In the last of the years given in this section, probably 876, we are to place the various bull and lion inscriptions, which in general agree with this portion of the Annals.[6] One of these bull inscriptions, as well as the text of the great altar, adds a good bit in regard to the hunting expeditions, which may be dated, so far as they can be dated at all, to this year.[7] Here too we must

[1]Le Gac, *Introd.*
[2]Le Gac, iii. [3]Ibid. 126f.
[4]Ibid, ii; 123f. (B).
[5]First mentioned as starting point of an expedition in 879, Ann. III. 1.
[6]Bulls 76, 77; Lions 809, 841. Budge-King, 189ff.; Le Gaċ, 181ff. Made up of brief attribution to king, then regular building text, then duplicates of Ann. III. 84ff.
[7]Bull 77; Budge-King, 201ff.; Peiser KB. I. 124f.; Altar, L. 43ff.; Le Gac, 171ff.

place the Mahir document,[1] describing the erection of a temple to that deity at Imgur Bel, as is shown by the specific reference to a campaign to the Lebanon for the purpose of securing cedar. The years 875-868 seem to have been years of peace, for the only reference we can attribute to them is an expedition to the Mehri land for beams to erect a temple at Nineveh[2] and so to this period we must assign the Ishtar bowl inscriptions.[3] Finally, we have the campaign of 867, the last fixed date in the reign of Ashur nasir apal, and the reason for compiling the latest edition of the Annals. For this year, and for this alone, this latest edition has the value of a strictly contemporaneous document.[4]

The last section of the Annals consists of the building account, found also in nearly all the other inscriptions, though naturally here it is in the form it last assumed. It may be seen in greater or less fulness in the so called Standard Inscription,[5] the short account so monotonously repeated on the slabs at Kalhu and so familiar to all who have visited any Museum where Assyrian antiquities are preserved. There seem to be two recen-

[1] V R. 69f.; Budge-King, TSBA. VII. 59ff.; Budge-King, 167ff. S. A. Strong, RP², IV. 83ff.; Harper, 29ff.
[2] Ann. III. 91f.
[3] III R. 3, 10; Budge-King, 158ff.; S. A. Strong, RP², II. 95.
[4] Ann. III. 92ff.
[5] L. 1ff.; Schrader, *Inschrift Asur-nasir-abals;* Talbot, *Proc. Soc. Antiquaries of Scotland,* VI. 198ff.; Meissner, *Chestomathie,* 7f.; Abel-Winckler, 6. RP¹, VII. 11ff.; Ward, *Proc. Amer. Oriental Soc.,* X. xcix; Budge-King, 212ff.; Le Gac, 153ff. The number of slabs containing this inscription which may be found in the various Museums of Europe and America is simply amazing. No full collection or collation of these has ever been made. Many are still exposed to the destructive effects of the atmosphere at Nimrud and are rapidly being ruined. Squeezes of these were taken by the Cornell Expedition. Others at Ashur, MDOG., xxi. 52; KTA. 25. Several are in the newly opened section of the Constantinople Museum, cf. Bezold, *Ztf. f. Keilschriftforschung,* I. 269. An unknown number is in the British Museum, and were utilized by Budge-King, l. c. Streck, ZA. XIX. 258, lists those published from European Museums. These are Edinburgh, Talbot l. c.; Copenhagen, Knudtzon, ZA. XII. 256; St. Petersburg, Jeremias, ZA. I. 49; Bucharest, D. H. Müller, *Wiener Ztf. f. Kunde d. Morgenlandes,* XIII. 169ff.; Dresden,

sions, a longer and a shorter,[1] and some, to judge from the variations in the references, are much later than 880. The same inscription essentially is also found as the ending of the Ishtar, Mahir, Calah Palace,[2] Calah wall,[3] Bulls, and Ninib inscriptions.[4] Variants are few, but are not without value in fixing the relative dates of the various recensions. For example, some of the Standard inscriptions, as well as the Ishtar and Mahir ones, insert a reference to "Mount Lebanon and the Great Sea" which would place them after 876, and this is confirmed by the reference to Liburna of Patina which occurs in the Annals and the Calah wall inscription. Of course, this gives only the

Jeremias, *l. c.;* Zürich, Bezold, *Literatur,* 71; Cannes, Le Gac, ZA. IX. 390; Lyons, Ley, RT. XVII. 55; Rome, O. Marucchi, *Museo Egizio Vaticano,* 334; Bezold, ZA. II. 229. In addition, there are, according to Budge-King, *l. c.,* copies at Paris, Berlin, Munich, the Hague, etc. For the Berlin inscriptions, cf. *Verzeichnis der vorderasiatischen Altertümer,* 92ff.; 101. No less than 59 are known to have been or to be in America. The majority have been listed by Ward, *op. cit.,* xxxv, and Merrill, *ibid.* xci. ff.: cf. *Bibliotheca Sacra.* xxxii. 320ff. Twelve in the possession of the New York Historical Society have not been on exhibition since the society moved into its new quarters, and are completely inaccessible, the statements in the guide books to the contrary notwithstanding. The Andover slab is published by Merrill, *op. cit.* lxxiii, and the one from Amherst by Ward, *l. c.* These were presented by Rawlinson and Layard to missionaries, and by them to the institutions named, as were the following: Yale University; Union College, Schenectady; Williams College; Dartmouth College; Middlebury College; Bowdoin College; Auburn (N. Y.) Theological Seminary; Connecticut Historical society at Hartford; Meriden (Conn.) Public Library; Theological Seminary of Virginia; Mercantile Library of St. Louis. An inscribed relief to which my attention has been called by Professor Allan Marquand, has been presented by Mr. Garrett to Princeton University. Three similar slabs, loaned by the late Mr. J. P. Morgan, are in the Metropolitan Museum in New York City.—In this place we may also note the brick inscriptions in America, listed by Merrill, *l. c.,* as well as the statute inscription, III R. 4, 8; Menant, 65; Schrader, *Keilinschriften und das Alte Testament,*[2] 184.

[1] Le Gac, xvii.
[2] Budge-King, 173ff.; Le Gac, 188ff.
[3] Budge-King, 177ff.
[4] Budge-King, 209ff.

upper limit, for it would be dangerous to suggest a lower one in the case of documents which copy so servilely. Some of the Standard inscriptions, as well as the Bulls, have a reference to Urartu, of great importance as the first in any literature to the country which was soon to become the worthy rival of Assyria. Absence of such reference in the regular Annals is pretty conclusive evidence that there were no warlike relations, so that these too are to be dated after 876. With this is to be compared the addition telling of the conquest of Nairi, found in the Ishtar, Mahir, and Calah Palace inscriptions, and which would seem to refer to the same period. The Suhi, Laqe, and Sirqu reference, through its omission in the Monolith, is also of value as adding proof that that inscription dates to 880.[1]

Much the same situation as regards the sources is found in the reign of his son Shalmaneser III (860-825). Aside from a few minor inscriptions, our main source is again the official account which has come down to us in several recensions of different date. The process by which these recensions were made is always the same. The next earlier edition was taken as a basis, and from this were extracted, generally in the exact words of the original, such facts as seemed of value to the compiler. When the end of this original was reached, and it was necessary for the editor to construct his own narrative, the recital becomes fuller, and, needless to say, becomes also a better source. If, then, we have the original from which the earliest portion of a certain document was copied or abstracted, we must entirely cast aside the copy in favor of the contemporary writing. This would appear self evident, but failure to observe this distinction has led to more than one error in the history of the reign.[2]

[1]Minor inscriptions, L. 83f.; G. Smith, *Disc.*, 76; Budge-King, 155ff.; Le Gac, 172; the very fragmentary Obelisk, Le Gac, 207ff.; KTA. 25; MDOG. 20, 21ff.; 21, 15ff. King, *Supplement*, no. 192, 470, 1805. Hommel. *Zwei Jagdinschriften*, 1879, with photographs; Andrä, *Tempel*, 86ff.

[2]The majority of the inscriptions for the reign were first given in Layard, *Inscriptions*, and in the Rawlinson publication, cf. for first working over, Rawlinson, JRAS. OS. XII. 431ff. The edition of Amiaud-Scheil, *Les inscriptions de Salmanasar II*, 1890, though without cunei-

Each of these editions ends with the account of some important campaign, the need of writing up which was the reason for the collection of the events of previous years which were not in themselves worthy of special commemoration. The first of these is the one which ends with the famous battle of Qarqara in 854. This has come down to us in a monumental copy which was set up at Kirkh, the ancient Tushhan, and which has been named the Monolith inscription.[1] For the events of 860-854, then, we need go no further than this, for it is strictly contemporaneous with the events it describes. No actual errors can be pointed out in it, a seeming distortion of the chronology being due simply to the desire of the scribe to indicate the unity of two campaigns, carried out in different years, but against the same country.[2] How moderate are its numbers is shown by comparing its 14,000 killed at Qarqara with the 20,500 of the Obelisk, the 25,000 of the Bulls, and the 29,000 of the recently discovered statue from Ashur. As we shall see below, it is correct in giving no campaign for 855, though the Bulls inscription, written a generation later, has not hesitated to fill the gap. This is the only edition which seems to be entirely original and a comparison with those which are in large part compilations is favorable to it in every way. In fact, the oft repeated reproach as to the catalogue nature of the Shalmaneser writings is due to the taking of the Obelisk as a fair sample, whereas it stands at the other extreme, that of a document almost entirely made up by abridgement of other documents, and so can hardly be expected to retain much of the literary flavor of its originals. The Mono-

form text, is still valuable on account of its arrangement by years, as well as of its full notes, cf. also Winckler-Peiser, KB. I. 128ff. The one edition which is up to date is N. Rasmussen, *Salmanasser den II's Indskriften*, 1907, though the same may be said of the selections in Rogers, 293ff.

[1] III R 7f; Rasmussen, 1ff.; 2ff. Photograph, Rogers, 537; *Hist.*, op. 226. Amiaud-Scheil, *passim;* Peiser, KB. I. 150ff. Menant, 105ff.; Sayce, RP[1], III. 83ff.; Scheil, RP[2], IV. 55ff.; Craig, *Hebraica*, III. 201ff.; Harper, 33ff.; cf. Jastrow, AJSL. IV. 244ff.
[2] II. 66.

lith, on the other hand, free from the necessity of abridging, will hold its own in literary value with the other historical writings of the Assyrians.

The next edition was prepared in 851, at the conclusion of the Babylonian expedition. The document as a whole is lost, but we have excerpts in the Balawat inscription.[1] For the years 859, 857, and 856, the excerpts are very brief, but fortunately this is of no importance as we have their originals in the Monolith. No mention is made of the years following until 852-851 which are described so fully that we may believe we have here the actual words of the document. It is interesting to notice that there is no particular connection between the reliefs on the famous bronzes[2] and the inscription which accompanies them. The latter ends in 851, the pictures go on to 849. The more conspicious pictures were brought up to date, but, for the inscription which few would read, a few extracts, borrowed from the edition of two years previous, sufficed. Incidentally, it shows us that no new edition had been made in those two years. For the years before 853, the practical loss of this edition need trouble us little as it seems merely to have copied the original of the Monolith. That it might have had some slight value in restoring the text of that lost original seems indicated by a hint of a fuller text in one place[3] and a more moderate number of enemies slaughtered in another.[4] For the events of 853, as given in this

[1]Pinches, PSBA. VII. 89ff.; *The Bronze Ornaments of the Palace Gates of Balawat*, 1880; Rasmussen, XIff.; Amiaud-Scheil, *passim;* Delitzsch, *Beitr. z. Assyr.*, VI. 133ff.; Winckler KB. I. 134ff. Scheil, RP², IV. 74ff.

[2]Pinches, *Bronze Ornaments*, a magnificent publication. A cheaper edition of the reliefs, with valuable analysis of and comments on the sculptures, Billerbeck; *Beitr. z. Assyr.* VI. 1ff. Additional reliefs owned by G. Schlumberger, Lenormant, *Gazette Arch.*, 1878 pl. 22ff. and p. 119ff. Still others, de Clerq, *Catalogue*, II 183ff., quoted Billerbeck, 2. I have not yet seen King, *Bronze Reliefs from the Gates of Shalmaneser*, 1915.

[3]II. 6f.

[4]Balawat kills but 300 while Monolith slaughters 3400.

edition, we have only the abstract of it in the Bulls inscription.[1]

The year 845, the year of the expedition to the sources of the Tigris, seems to mark the end of a third period, commemorated by a third edition, extracts from which are given in the inscriptions on the Bulls.[2] That it actually began with the year 850 is shown by the use of a new system of dating, by the king's year and the number of the Euphrates crossing. Comparison with passages preserved in the Balawat extracts shows that the work of excerpting has been badly done by the editor of the third edition. The capture of Lahiru is placed in the wrong year,[3] the graphical error of Ukani for Amukkani shows it derived from the Balawat edition, while variations between the two copies of the bull inscription indicate that we cannot be sure of the exact words of the original.[4] And we can also point to deliberate falsification in the insertion of an expedition to Kashiari against Anhitti of Shupria, when the older edition, the Monolith, knew of no expedition for the year 855. It has already been shown elsewhere that this is closely connected with the attempt of the turtanu (prime minister) Dan Ashur to date his accession to power to 856 instead of 854, and to hide the fact of the palace revolution which seems to have marked the year 855.[5]

From various hints, it is possible to prove that a fourth edition was prepared in 837, the end of the wars with Tabal. The most striking evidence for this is the fact that, after this year, the Obelisk suddenly becomes much fuller, a clear proof that the author knew that he was now dealing with events not previously written up. We may see, then, in the Obelisk account from 844 to 837 an abstract of the lost edition of 837. But we are not con-

[1] Bull 75ff.
[2] Discovery, Layard, NR. I. 59. L. 12ff.; 46f.; Rasmussen, XVff.; 42ff. Amiaud-Scheil, *passim;* Delitzsch, *op. cit.*, 144ff.; Menant, 113ff.
[3] Bull 79; cf. Balawat IV. 6.
[4] Variants in Amiaud-Scheil, *passim.* The most striking is the different text with which they end, cf. Amiaud-Scheil, 58 n. 1.
[5] Cf. below under the Obelisk, and, for fuller discussion, Olmstead, *Jour. Amer. Or. Soc.* XXXIV. 346f.

ASSYRIAN HISTORIOGRAPHY 25

fined to this. One actual fragment of this edition is the fragment which deals with the events of 842 and is so well known because of its reference to Jehu.[1] The first half of this is also intercalated after the introduction to one of the Bull inscriptions, and before year four, thus showing that it was inserted to bring the edition of 845 up to date.[2] Based on this edition, though only in very brief abstract, seems also the so called throne inscription from Ashur, whose references to Damascus, Que, Tabal, and Melidi form a group which can best be correlated with the events of the years 839, 840, 838, and 837, respectively.[3] Another Ashur inscription on a royal statute gives selections from the events of the reign, up to 835, but its main source is evidently the same.[4]

But the strongest proof of the existence of this edition is to be found in the two fragments of clay tablets which are not, like all the preceding, epigraphical copies of the originals, but form part of the original itself.[5] These two bits are written in the cursive style, and, though their discoverer believed them to belong to separate documents, the fact that one so closely supplements the other, and that they have the same common relation to the other editions, justifies us in assuming that they really do belong together. At first sight, it might be argued that they are to be restored from the text of the Obelisk, with which they often agree verbally. Closer inspection shows, however, that they contain matter which is not found in that monument, and that therefore they belong to an earlier and fuller edition, yet the

[1] III R. 5, 6; Rasmussen, XXI; 56; Delitzsch, *Assyr. Lesestücke*[4], 51f. Amiaud-Scheil, 58; Winckler, KB. I. 140; Ungnad, I. 112; Rogers, 303f.
[2] L. 12f.; Rasmussen, XIX; 53.
[3] Discovery, Layard, NR. II. 46ff.; cf. G. Smith, TSBA. I. 77. L. 76f.; Craig, *Hebraica*, II 140ff.; Rasmussen, XXXVIII; 84ff.; Amiaud-Scheil, 74ff.; Delitzsch, *Beitr. z. Assyr.*, VI. 152f.; cf. Jastrow, *Hebraica*, V. 230ff.
[4] Andrä, MDOG. 21, 20ff.; 39ff.; Delitzsch, *ibid.* 52; KTA. 30; Langdon, *Expository Times*, XXIII, 69; Rogers, 298f.; 529.
[5] Boissier, RT. XXV. 82ff.

resemblance to the Obelisk is so close that they cannot be much earlier. On the other hand, the Bulls inscription can be compared for the events of 854-852 and this has all that our tablets have, plus a good bit more. They therefore belong between these two editions, and the only time we can place them is 837. Since the clay tablets so fully abstract the Bulls inscription wherever the latter is available for comparison, we may assume that in 857-855 they give the minimum of that inscription. Thus we have the editions of 845, of 837, and of 829, in a common line of descent. Although for 857-856, there are numerous verbal coincidences with the Balawat excerpts, it must be noted that not all the plus of our tablets appears in that document, and we can only assume a common source, a conclusion which well agrees with our characterization of the Balawat inscription as a series of mere extracts. That this common source was also the source of the Monolith seems proved by a certain similarity of phraseology as well as by the reference to Tiglath Pileser in connection with Pitru, but this similarity is not great enough fully to restore our plus passages. Unfortunately for the student of history, our tablets do not add any new facts, for, in the parts preserved, we already had the earlier representatives of the original sources from which the edition was derived. It does, however, throw a most interesting light on the composition and development of these sources.

Last and least valuable of all is the Obelisk.[1] Because of its most interesting sculptures and because it gives a summary of almost the entire reign, it has either been given the place of honor, or a place second to the Monolith alone. The current

---

[1]Discovery at Kalhu, Layard, NR. II. 282. Layard, *Monuments of Nineveh*, I. 53ff.; L. 87ff.; Abel-Winckler, 7f; Rasmussen, XXXIIIff.; 80ff. Amiaud-Scheil, *passim*; Winckler, KB. I. 128ff. Oppert, *Expéd.* I. 342; *Hist.* 108ff.; Menant, 97ff.; Sayce, RP¹, V. 29ff.; Scheil, RP², IV. 38; Jastrow, *Hebraica*, V. 230. Mengedoht, *Bab. Or. Rec.*, VIII, 111ff.; 141ff.; 169ff. Photographs and drawings too frequent for notice. Casts are also common, e. g., in America, Metropolitan Museum, N. Y. City; University of Pennsylvania; Haskell Museum, University of Chicago; Boston Museum of Fine Arts.

view is given by one of our most prominent Assyriologists as follows: "The first rank must be ascribed to the Black Obelisk, and for the reason that it covers a greater period of Shalmaneser's reign than any other.... It is clear then, that for a study of the reign of Shalmaneser II the black obelisk must form the starting point, and that, in direct connection with it, the other inscriptions may best be studied, grouping themselves around it as so many additional fragmentary manuscripts would around the more complete one which we hit upon, for a fundamental text."[1]

This view might be accepted were the problem one of the "lower criticism". Unfortunately, it is clearly one for the "higher" and accordingly we should quote the Black Obelisk only when an earlier edition has not been preserved. There is no single point where, in comparison with an earlier one, there is reason to believe that it has the correct text, in fact, it is, as might be expected in the case of a show inscription, filled with mistakes, many of which were later corrected, while in one case the engraver has been forced to erase entire lines.[2] Its date is 829, a whole generation later than the facts first related, and it can be shown that it is a formal apology for the turtanu (prime minister), Dan Ashur, glorifies him at the expense of his monarch, and attempts to conceal the palace revolution which marked his coming into power by changing the date of his eponomy from 854 to 856 and by filling in the year 855 with another event. Nor is it without bearing in this connection that it was prepared in 829, the very year in which the revolt of Ashur dan apal broke out as a protest against the control of his father by the too powerful turtanu.[3] As these last years of the reign were years of revolt, there is no reason for believing that there was another edition prepared, and the narrative of this revolt in the Annals of his son Shamshi Adad points in the same direction.

[1] Jastrow, *l. c.*
[2] Cf. the textual commentary in Amiaud-Scheil, *passim*, and especially 65 n. 6.
[3] Cf. Olmstead, *Jour. Amer. Or. Soc.*, *l. c.*

Of documents which do not belong to this connected series, the most important is the recently discovered lion inscription from Til Barsip. Aside from its value in identifying the site of that important city and an extra detail or two, its importance is not great, as it is the usual type of display inscription.[1] The Tigris Tunnel inscription also has its main importance from the locality in which it was found.[2] Other brief inscriptions add a bit as to the building operations, which, curiously enough, are neglected in the official annals series.[3]

[1] R. C. Thompson, PSBA. XXXIV. 66ff.; cf. Hogarth, *Accidents of an Antiquary's Life*, op. 175.
[2] Scheil, RT. XXII. 38.
[3] L. 77f.; Amiaud-Scheil, 78; Rasmussen, XLI; 88f. Layard, NR. II. 46; I. 281. Bricks in America, Merrill, *Proc. Amer. Or. Soc.*, X. c; *Bibl. Sacra*. XXXII. 337ff.; Streck, *Ztf. Deutsch. Morg. Gesell.*, 1908, 758; Scheil, RT. XXVI. 35ff.; Pinches, PSBA. XXXII. 49f., of year I; KTA. 26ff.; 77; MDOG. 21, 20f.; 22, 29ff.; 22, 77; 28, 24f.; 31, 15; 32, 15ff.; 36, 16ff.; 48, 27; Andrä, *Tempel*, 41ff.; Taf. XX. XXIIf.

CHAPTER IV

SHAMSHI ADAD AND THE SYNCHRONISTIC HISTORY

The main source for the reign of Shamshi Adad (825-812) is the official Annals which exists in two recensions. One, written in archaistic characters, from the south east palace at Kalhu, has long been known. After the usual introduction, it deals briefly with the revolt of Ashur dan apal. No attempt is made to differentiate the part which deals with his father's reign from that of his own, and the single paragraph which is devoted to it gives us no real idea of its importance or of its duration. Then follow four expeditions, the first two given very briefly, the last rather fully. As the years of the reign are not indicated, there is considerable difficulty in obtaining a satisfactory chronology.[1] The other carries the record two years further, but has not yet been published.[2]

The long list of expeditions which the Assyrian Chronicle attributes to the reign of Adad nirari (812-783) indicates that he must have composed Annals, but they have not as yet been discovered. Of extant inscriptions, the earliest is probably that on the statue base of Sammuramat (Semiramis), in which she is placed before her son and emphasis is laid on the fact that she is the widow of Shamshi Adad rather than that she is the mother of the reigning monarch.[3] Next in time comes the inscription on the famous Nabu statue in which Adad nirari is placed first,

[1] IR. 29ff. Scheil, *Inscription Assyr. Archaïque de Samsi Ramman IV*, 1889. Abel, KB. I. 174ff. Oppert, *Hist.*, 122ff.; Menant, 119ff.; Sayce, RP1, I. 11ff.; Harper, 45ff. For errors in writing cf. Scheil, VI; for use of rare words, *ibid.* VII.

[2] MDOG. 28, 31f. Through the courtesy of Dr. Andrä, I was permitted to see this in the excavation house at Ashur in 1908.—Cf. also the palace brick, Scheil, RT. XXII. 37.

[3] MDOG. 40, 24ff. 42, 34ff.

but with Sammuramat at his side, and which accordingly marks the decline of the queen mother's power.[1] Near the end of his reign must be placed the two Kalhu inscriptions in which Sammuramat is not mentioned. One refers to the conquests from the sea of the rising sun to the sea of the setting sun, a statement which would be possible only after the conquest of Kis in 786. This is the document which throws a vivid light on the early history of Assyria, but the remainder is lost[2] and a duplicate adds nothing new.[3] The other Kalhu inscription adds considerable material, but in a condensed form which makes it most difficult to locate the facts in time. The historical portion is divided into three sections which seem roughly to correspond with the chronological order. First comes a list of the peoples conquered on the eastern frontier, arranged geographically from south to north. As but two of these names are listed in the Assyrian Chronicle, and as each occurs several times, it is impossible to locate them exactly in time. The second section deals in considerable detail with an expedition against Damascus but the Chronicle does not list one even against central Syria. The fulness of this account shows that it took place not far from the subjugation of Kaldi land, the narrative of which ends the document and shows it to have been written not far from 786, its date in the Chronicle.[4]

For the remaining reigns of the dynasty, we have only the data in the Assyrian Chronicle. No annals or in fact any other inscription has come down to us, and, so far at least as the

[1] Rawlinson, *Monarchies*, II. 118 n. 7; Photograph, Rogers, 511; *Religion*, op. 86; I. R. 35, 2; Abel-Winckler, 14; Abel, KB. I. 192f.; Rogers, 307f.; Winckler, *Textbuch*³, 27f.; Meissner, *Chrestomathie*, 10; Menant, 127f.
[2] Layard, NR. II. 20. L. 70; I. R. 35, 3; Delitzsch, *Lesestücke*², 99; Abel-Winckler, 13. Abel, KB. I. 188ff. Sayce, RP¹, I. 3ff.; S. A. Strong, RP², IV. 88f.; Harper, 50f.
[3] L. 70.
[4] Rawlinson, *Athenaeum*, 1856, 174; I R. 35, 1; Winckler, *Textbuch*³, 26f. Abel, KB. I. 190ff.; Ungnad, I. 112f.; Rogers, 306f. Talbot, JRAS. XIX. 182ff.; Harper, 51f.; Meissner, *Chrestomathie*, 9; Menant, 126f.—Nineveh brick, I R. 35, 4. Abel, KB. I. 188f. Ashur inscriptions, KTA. 35f.; MDOG. 22, 19; 26, 62.

ASSYRIAN HISTORIOGRAPHY

annals are concerned, there is little likelihood of their discovery, as there is no reason to believe that any were composed in this period of complete decline. But, curiously enough, from this very period comes the document which throws the most light on the earliest period of Assyrian expansion, the so called Synchronistic history.[1] Adad nirari is the last ruler mentioned, but the fact that he is named in the third person shows that it was compiled not earlier than the reign of his successor Shalmaneser IV.

Our present copy is a tablet from the library of a later king, seemingly Ashur bani apal.[2] In form, it marks an advance over any historical document we have thus far studied, for it is an actual history for many centuries of the relations between Assyria and Babylonia. But it is as dry as possible, for only the barest facts are given, with none of the mass of picturesque details which we have learned to expect in the annals of the individual kings. Nevertheless, its advance over preceding documents should not be over estimated. Its emphasis on treaties and boundaries has led to the idea that it was compiled from the archives as a sort of diplomatic pièce justificative in a controversy with Babylonia over the possession of a definite territory.[3] Its true character, however, is clearly brought out in its closing words "A succeeding prince whom they shall establish in the land of Akkad, victory and conquest may he write down, and on this inscribed stone (naru), eternal and not to be forgotten, may he [add it]. Whoever takes it, may he listen to all that is written, the majesty of the land of Ashur may he worship continually. As for Shumer and Akkad, their sins may he expose to all the regions of the world."[4]

[1] II R. 65, 1; III R. 4, 3; Winckler, *Untersuch.*, 148ff.; CT. XXXVI. 38ff.; cf. the introduction of Budge-King; King, *Tukulti Ninib*. Peiser-Winckler, KB. I. 194ff.; G. Smith, *Disc.* 250f.; Sayce, TSBA. II. 119ff.; RP1, III. 29ff.; RP2, IV. 24ff.; Barta in Harper, 196; cf. Winckler, AOF. I. 114ff.; Belck, *Beitr. Geog. Gesch.*, I. 5ff.
[2] Maspero, *Hist.*, II. 595, dates its composition to this reign.
[3] Peiser-Winckler, KB. I. 194 n. 1.
[4] IV. 22ff.

Obviously, then, this tablet of clay is only a copy of an earlier *naru* or memorial inscription on stone, and we should expect it to be only the usual display inscription. This is still further proved by the introduction, mutilated as it is, "...to the god Ashur...his prayer...before his face I speak....eternally a [tablet] with the mention....the majesty and victory [which the kings of Ashur mad]e, they conquered all, [the march] of former [expedi]tions, who conquered.....[their booty to their lands they br]ought..." Clearly, this is the language of a display inscription and not of a diplomatic pièce justificative. So we can consider our document not even a history in the true sense of the word, merely an inscription erected to the glory of Ashur and of his people, but with the "sins of Shumer and Akkad," in other words, with the wars of the Babylonians against "the land"[1] and with the sinful destruction of Assyrian property they caused, also in mind. When we take this view, we are no longer troubled by the numerous mistakes, even to the order of the kings, which so greatly reduce the value of the document where its testimony is most needed.[2] We can understand such "mistakes" in a display inscription, exposed to view in a place where it would not be safe for an individual to point out the truth. But that it could have been used as a pièce justificative, with all its errors, when the Babylonians could at once have refuted it, is incredible.

The accession of Tiglath Pileser IV (745-728) marks a return to warfare, and the consequent prosperity is reflected in an increase of the sources both in quantity and in quality.[3] Tiglath Pileser prepared for the walls of his palace a series of annals, in three recensions, marked by the number of lines to the slab, seven, twelve, or sixteen, and seemingly by little else. Originally they adorned the walls of the central palace at Kalhu,

---

[1] Cf. Belck, *Beitr. Geog. Gesch. I.* 5ff.—The double mention of Ashur bel kala and Shalmaneser points to double sources, one the original of BM. 27859, Peiser, OLZ. XI. 141.

[2] Cf. Winckler, AOF. I. 109ff.

[3] For inscriptions of reign, cf. Rost, *Keilschrifttexte Tiglat-Pilesers III;* cf. also Anspacher, *Tiglath Pileser,* 1ff.

but Esarhaddon, a later king of another dynasty, defaced many of the slabs and built them into his south west palace. Thus, even with the three different recensions, a large part of the Annals has been lost forever. For years, the great problem of the reign of Tiglath Pileser was the proper chronological arrangement of this inscription. Thanks to the aid of the Assyrian Chronicle, it is now fairly fixed, though with serious gaps. Once they are arranged, little further criticism is needed, for they are the usual type, rather dry and uninteresting to judge from the extant fragments.[1] Perhaps separate notice should be given to the sculptured slabs in Zürich with selections from the Annals.[2]

Next to the Annals comes the clay tablet from Kalhu, from which, if we are to judge by the proportions, less than a half has survived.[3] Thus, owing to the method used by the Assyrians in turning the tablet for writing, only the first and last parts are preserved. Unfortunately, the greater part of what is preserved is taken up with an elaborate introduction and conclusion which we would gladly exchange for more strictly historical data. The other contents are, first an elaborate account of the wars in Babylonia, next of the wars on the Elamite frontier, a brief paragraph on Ulluba and Kirhu, and then the beginning of the war with Urartu. Each of these paragraphs is marked off by a line across the tablet. Thus far, it is clear, we have a geographical order for

[1]Detailed bibliography of the fragments, Anspacher, *Tiglath Pileser*, 3ff.; Discovery, Layard, NR. II. 300. L. 19ff.; III R. 9f. Rost, *de inscriptione Tiglat-Pileser III quae vocatur Annalium*, 1892; Rost, Iff.; 2ff.; Winckler, *Textbuch*3, 28ff. Ungnad I. 113ff.; Rogers, 313ff.; Schrader KB. II. 24ff.; Rodwell, RP1, V. 45ff.; Menant, 144ff. For discussion of arrangements of fragments, cf. G. Smith, *Ztf. f. Aegyptologie*, 1869, 9ff.; *Disc.*, 266; Schrader, *Keilschrift und Geschichtsforschung*, 395ff.; *Abh. Berl. Akad.*, 1880; Tiele, *Gesch.*, 224; Hommel, *Gesch.*, 648ff.

[2]Boissier, PSBA. I have not seen his *Notice sur quelque Monuments Assyr. a l'université de Zürich*, 1912.

[3]Usually called the Nimrud inscription, a cause of confusion. K. 3751. Photograph of obverse, but upside down, Rogers, 541; *History*, op. 267. II R. 67; Rost, XXXVff; 54ff. Schrader, KB. II. 8ff.; Erneberg, JA. VII. Ser. VI. 441ff.; Menant, 140ff.; Smith, *Disc,*, 256ff.; Strong, RP2, V. 115ff.; J. M. P. Smith, in Harper, 52ff.; Rogers, 322.

the paragraphs. After the break, we have an account of the Arab tribes on the border of Egypt. It is therefore clear that the order was continued in the break which must have contained the most of the Urartu account and whatever was said about Syria. The fulness with which the extant portion chronicles the Babylonian affairs makes it probable that the part now lost in the break dealt with Armenian and Syrian relations with equal fulness. The next paragraph seems to be a sort of summary of the various western rulers who had paid tribute, and the length of this list is another proof of the large amount lost. The very brief Tabal and Tyre paragraphs, out of the regular geographical order, are obvious postscripts and this dates them to year XVII (729), unless we are to assume that the scribe did not have them in mind when he wrote the reference to that year in the introduction. That they really did date to the next year, 728, is indicated by the fact that the Assyrian Chronicle seems to have had a Tyre expedition in that year.[1] If so, then our inscription must date from the last months of Tiglath Pileser's reign. Though written on clay, it is clearly a draft from which to engrave a display inscription on stone as it begins "Palace of Tiglath Pileser." The identity of certain passages[2] with the Nimrud slab shows close connection, but naturally the much fuller recital of the tablet is not derived from it. We have also a duplicate fragment from the Nabu temple at Kalhu and this is marked by obvious Babylonianisms.[3]

With the Nimrud clay tablet is easily confused the Nimrud slab.[4] This dates from 743 and is thus the earliest inscription from the reign. But its account is so brief that it is of but trifling value. It assists a little in conjecturing what is lost from the tablet and, mention of an event here is naturally of value as

[1] Cf. Olmstead, *Jour. Amer. Or. Soc.*, XXXIV. 357.
[2] I. 5, 9ff., 16, 22, 47.
[3] DT. 3. Schrader, *Abh. Berl. Akad.* 1880, 15ff., with photograph. For the Babylonian character, cf. Rost, 11.
[4] Layard, NR. II. 33. L. 17f. Schrader, KB. II. 2ff.; Rost, 42ff.; Oppert, *Exped.*, 336; Smith, *Disc.*, 271; Meissner, *Chrestomathie*, 10f.; Menant, 138ff.

establishing a minimum date. But where both have preserved the same account, the tablet is the fuller, and, in general, better, even though it is so much later.[1]

[1] Other inscriptions, III R. 10, 3, the place list; 83-1-18, 215, Winckler, AOF. II. 3f.; painted fragments, Layard, *Nineveh and Babylon*, 140f.

CHAPTER V

SARGON AND THE MODERN HISTORICAL CRITICISM

The scources for the reign of Sargon (722-705)[1] have already been discussed in detail elsewhere. All that is here needed is a summary of results.[2] They fall into three well marked groups. The first includes the early inscriptions of the reign, which are miscellaneous in character.[3] The circumstances under which Sargon came to the throne are indicated by a tablet from the second year which is of all the more value in that it is not a formal annals or display inscription.[4] The Nimrud inscription comes from Kalhu, the earliest capital of Sargon. Unfortunately, it is very brief and is not arranged in chronological order. Aside from the rather full account of Pisiris of Carchemish, sufficient to date the inscription soon after its capture, we have only the briefest of references, and its value would be nothing, could we only secure the original, perhaps the earliest edition of the Annals, on which it is based.[5] A brief fragment may be noted because of its mention of the sixth year, though we cannot be sure of the class to which it belongs.[6] Other fragments are either unpublished or of no importance.[7]

[1]Collected in Winckler, *Keilschrifttexte Sargons*, 1889.
[2]Olmstead, *Western Asia in the Days of Sargon of Assyria*, 1908, 1ff.
[3]*Sargon*, 17ff.
[4]K. 1349; Winckler, *Sammlung*, II. 1; AOF. I. 401ff.
[5]L. 33f.; Winckler, *Sargon*, I. 168ff.; II. 48; Lyon, *Assyr. Manual*, 9f.; Peiser, KB. II. 34ff.; Menant, 204ff.
[6]K. 1660; Winckler, *Sammlung*, II. 4.
[7]K. 221+2669; K. 3149; K. 3150; K. 4455; K. 4463, Winckler, *Sammlung*, II. 6; K. 4471, *ibid.* II. 4; DT. 310; 83-1-18, 215. The unpublished fragments known from Bezold, *Catalogue, ad loc.*

(36)

As a proved source for the second group, the newly discovered tablet should begin our study.[1] From the standpoint of source study, it is of exceptional value as it is strictly contemporaneous and yet gives a very detailed account in Annals form of the events of a single year. The tablet was "written", probably composed, though it may mean copied, by Nabu shallimshunu, the great scribe of the King, the very learned, the man of Sargon, the eldest son of Harmaki,—seemingly an Egyptian name,— and inhabitant of the city of Ashur. It was brought (before the God Ashur?) in the limmu or eponym year of Ishtar duri, 714-713, and tells us of the events of 714. It is written on an unusually large tablet of clay and is in the form of a letter. It begins "To Ashur the father of the gods... greatly, greatly may there be peace. To the gods of destiny and the goddesses who inhabit E har sag gal kurkurra, their great temple, greatly, greatly may there be peace. To the gods of destiny and the goddesses who inhabit the city of Ashur their great temple, greatly, greatly may there be peace. To the city and its inhabitants may there be peace. To the palace which is situated in the midst may there be peace. As for[2] Sargon the holy priest, the servant, who fears thy great godhead, and for his camp, greatly, greatly there is peace." So this looks like a letter from the king to the god Ashur, to the city named from him, and to its inhabitants. Yet it is a very unusual rescript, very different from those which have come down to us in the official archives, especially in the use of the third person in speaking of the king, while in the regular letters the first is always found. Further, in the body of the supposed letter, the king, as is usual in the official annals, speaks in the first person.

However it may be with the real character of the "letter," there can be no doubt as to its great value. To be sure, we may see in its boast that in the campaign but six soldiers were lost a more or less severe stretching of the truth, but, at least in com-

---

[1]Thureau-Dangin, *Relation de la Huitième Campagne de Sargon*, 1912.
[2]So Thureau-Dangin, *ad loc.*

parison with the later records, it is not only much fuller, but far more accurate. Indeed, comparison with the later Annals shows that document to be even worse than we had dared suspect.

Comparison of the newly discovered inscription with the parallel passages of the broken prism B shows that this is simply a condensed form of its original. The booty seems to have been closely copied, but the topographical details are much abbreviated. The discovery of this tablet, while supplying the lacunae in Prism B, has made this part useless. But all the more clearly is brought out the superiority, in this very section, of the Prism over the later Annals. Naturally, we assume the same to be true in the other portions preserved, in fact, the discovery of the tablet has been a brilliant confirmation of the proof long ago given that this was superior to the Annals.[1] Unfortunately but a part of these fragments has been published[2] and the difficulties in the way of copying these fragments have made many mistakes.[3] But a few of these fragments have as yet been translated or even discussed.[4] For all parts of the reign which they cover, save where we have the tablet, they are now clearly seen to be our best authorities, nearer in date to the events they chronicle and much freer from suspicion than the Annals. The most urgent need for the history of the reign is that the fragments which are still unpublished[5] should be published at once with a collation of those previously given. Even a translation and examination of the fragments already published would mark a considerable advance in our knowledge of the period.[6]

[1] Olmstead, *Sargon*, 11ff., with reconstruction of the order of the various fragments, as against Prasek, OLZ. XII. 117, who sharply attacked me "über den historischen wert den Stab zu brechen."

[2] Winckler, *Sargon*, II. 45ff.; cf. I. xif. Photograph, Ball, *Light from the East*, 185. Thureau-Dangin, *op. cit.*, 76ff.

[3] To judge by a comparison of Winckler's text with that prepared by King for Thureau-Dangin, *l. c.*

[4] Winckler, *Sargon*, I. 186f.; AOF. II. 71ff.; *Mitth. Vorderas. Gesell.*, 1898, 1, 53; Thureau-Dangin, *l. c.*

[5] Cf. Bezold, ZA. 1889, 411 n. 1.

[6] For detailed study of Prism B, cf. Olmstead, *l. c.*

Very similar to Prism B is our other broken prism, A.[1] Both were found at Nineveh[2] and this of itself proves a date some distance from the end of the reign when Sargon was established at Dur Sharruken.[3] Prism A is of much the same type as the other, in fact, when we see how the Ashdod expedition, begun in the one, can be continued in the other,[4] we are led to believe that the two had a similar text. If, however, the Dalta episode in each refers to the same event, then they had quite different texts in this part of the history. Which of the two is the earlier and more trustworthy, if they did not have identical texts, and what are their relative relations cannot be decided in their fragmentary state, but that they are superior to the Annals is clear. Like Prism B, Prism A is worthy of better treatment and greater attention than it has yet been given.

The third group consists of the documents from about the year 707, which have come down to us inscribed on the walls of Sargon's capital, Dur Sharruken.[5] The earliest document of this group is naturally the inscription of the cylinders which were deposited as corner stones,[6] indeed, it closely agrees with the deed of gift which dated to 714.[7] The same inscription is also found on slabs.[8] It is the fullest and best account of the building of Dur Sharruken, and from it the other documents of the group seem to have derived their building recital. Nor are other phases of the culture life neglected, as witness, for example, the well

[1]Winckler, *Sargon*, II. 44; I. 186ff.; *Untersuch. Altor. Gesch.*, 118ff.; *Textbuch*³, 41f.; Rogers, 329f.; G. Smith, *Disc.*, 288ff. Boscawen, *Bab. Or. Rec.* IV. 118ff. The Dalta episode and the beginning and end are still untranslated.
[2]G. Smith, *Disc.*, 147.
[3]Cf. Olmstead, *Sargon*, 14 n.
[4]As in Winckler, *Sargon*, I. 186ff.
[5]For discussion of this group, cf. Olmstead, *Sargon*, 6ff.
[6]Place, *Nineve*, II. 291ff.; Oppert, *Dour Sarkayan*, 11ff.; I R. 36; Lyon, *Keilschrifttexte Sargons*, 1ff. Winckler, *Sargon*, II. 43; Menant, 199ff.; Peiser, KB. II. 38ff. Barta, in Harper, 59ff.
[7]Cf. Olmstead, *Sargon*, 178f.
[8]Menant, RT. XIII. 194.

known attempt to fix prices and lower the high cost of living by royal edict.

The remaining inscriptions of the group are all closely related and all seem derived from the Annals. The display inscription gives the data of the Annals in briefer form and in geographical order. Numbers are very much increased, and its only value is in filling the too numerous lacunæ of its original.[1] Imperfect recognition of its character has led many astray.[2] Other inscriptions of the group are incised on bulls, on foundaslabs, on bricks, pottery, and glass, or as labels on the sculptures. Save for the last, they are of absolutely no value for the historian as they simply abstract from the Annals. As for the Cyprus stole, its location alone gives it a factitious importance.[3]

The one important document of the group, then, is the Annals. That, with all its value, it is a very much over estimated document, has already been shown.[4] There are four recensions, some of which differ widely among themselves and from other inscriptions. For example, there are three accounts of the fate of Merodach Baladan. In one, he is captured;[5] in the second he begs for peace;[6] in the third, he runs away and escapes.[7] Naturally, we are inclined to accept the last, which is actually confirmed by the later course of events.

But it is only when we compare the Annals with earlier documents that we realize how low it ranks, even among official in-

[1]Botta, *Mon. de Nineve*, 95ff.; Winckler, *Sargon*, II. 30ff.; I. 97ff. Oppert-Menant, *Fastes de Sargon*.-JA. 1863ff.; Menant. 180ff.; Oppert, RP¹, IX. 1ff.; Peiser, KB. II. 52ff.

[2]The error in connecting Piru and Hanunu, for example, already pointed out by Olmstead, *Sargon*, 10, is still held by S. A. Cook, art. Philistines, in the new *Encyclopedia Britannica*.

[3]For full bibliography of the minor inscriptions, cf. Olmstead, *Sargon*, 6f. For others since found at Ashur, cf. KTA. 37-42; 71; MDOG. 20, 24; 22, 37; 25, 28, 31; 35; 26, 22; 31, 47; Andrä, *Tempel*, 91ff.; Taf. XXI; Genouillac-Thureau-Dangin, RA. X. 83ff.

[4]Olmstead, *Sargon*, 3ff.
[5]Display 133.
[6]Annals V.
[7]Annals 349.

scriptions. Already we have learned the dubious character of its chronology. The Assyrian Chronicle has "in the land" for 712, that is, there was no campaign in that year. Yet for that very year, the Annals has an expedition against Asia Minor! It is prism B which solves the puzzle. In the earliest years, it seems to have had the same chronology as the Annals. Later, it drops a year behind and, at the point where it ends, it has given the Ashdod expedition as two years earlier than the Annals.[1] Even with the old data, it was clear that the Prism was earlier and therefore probably more trustworthy; and it was easy to explain the puzzle by assuming that years "in the land" had been later padded out by the Annals, just as we have seen was done for Dan Ashur under Shalmaneser III. Now the discovery of the tablet of the year 714 has completely vindicated the character of Prism B while it has even more completely condemned the Annals as a particularly untrustworthy example of annalistic writing.

In the first place, it shows us how much we have lost. The tablet has 430 lines, of which a remarkably small portion consists of passages which are mere glorifications or otherwise of no value. Out of this mass of material, the Annals has utilized but 36 lines. That this is a fair sample of what we have lost in other years is hardly too much to suspect. Further, it would seem that the Annals used, not the tablet itself, but, since it has a phrase common to the Annals and the Prism,[2] but not found in the tablet, either the Prism itself or a common ancestor.

The cases where we can prove that the editor of the Annals "improved" his original are few but striking. It is indeed curious that he has in a few cases lowered the numbers of his original, even to the extent of giving three fortified cities and twenty four villages[3] where the tablet has twelve fortified cities and eighty four villages.[4] On the other hand, by a trick especially common among the Sargonide scribes, the 1,235 sheep of

[1]Cf. Olmstead, *Sargon*, 11.
[2]Ann. 125f.; Prism B, Thureau-Dangin, *op. cit.*, 76f.
[3]Ann. 105.
[4]Tabl. 89.

the tablet[1] has reached the enormous total of 100,225![2] More serious, because less likely to be allowed for, is the statement that Parda was captured[3] when the original merely says that it was abandoned by its chief.[4] But the most glaring innovation of the scribe is where, in speaking of the fate of Rusash, the Haldian king, after his defeat, he adds "with his own iron dagger, like a pig, his heart he pierced, and his life he ended."[5] This has long been doubted on general principles,[6] but now we have the proof that it is only history as the scribe would like it to have been written. For the new inscription, while giving the conventional picture of the despair of the defeated king, says not a word of any suicide.[7] However, the tablet does elsewhere mention the sickness of Rusash,[8] and it may well be that it is to this sickness that we must attribute his death later.[9] The complete misunderstanding of the whole campaign by earlier writers[10] furnishes the clearest indication of the unsatisfactory character of our recital so long as we must rely entirely on the Annals. It is the discovery of conditions like these which forces us to subject our official inscriptions to the most rigid scrutiny before we dare use them in our history.[11]

[1]Tabl. 349.
[2]Ann. 129; cf. Thureau-Dangin, *op. cit.*, 68, n. 4 for comparison of numbers. The same phenomenon can be constantly seen in the huge increases of the numbers of the Display inscription as compared with its original, the Annals.
[3]Ann. 106.
[4]Tabl. 84.
[5]Ann. 139.
[6]Cf. Olmstead, *Sargon*, 111.
[7]Tabl. 411ff.
[8]*Ibid.* 115.
[9]Cf. Thureau-Dangin, *op. cit.*, xix.
[10]Compare, for example, the brief and inaccurate account in Olmstead, *Sargon*, 112ff., with that in Thureau-Dangin, *op. cit.* on the basis of the new tablet.
[11]Botta, *Monuments de Ninive*, pl. 70ff.; 104ff.; 158ff.; Winckler, *Sargon* II. pl. 1ff. Oppert in Place, *Ninive*, II. 309ff.; *Les Inscriptions de Dour Sarkayan*, 29ff.; RP[1] VII. 21ff.; Menant, 158ff.; Winckler, *De inscriptione quae vocatur Annalium*, 1886; *Sargon*, I. 3ff.

CHAPTER VI

ANNALS AND DISPLAY INSCRIPTIONS

(Sennacherib and Esarhaddon)

Of the sources for the reign of Sennacherib (705-686),[1] the chief is the Annals, added to at intervals of a few years, and so existing in several editions. As usual, the latest of these, the Taylor inscription, has been accorded the place of honor, so that the earliest edition, the so called Bellino Cylinder, can be called by a well known historian "a sort of duplicate of" the Taylor inscription.[2] As we have seen repeatedly, the exact reverse should be our procedure, though here, as in the case of Ashur nasir apal, the evil results in the writing of history are less serious than in the case of most reigns. This is due to the unusual circumstances that, with comparatively few exceptions, there was little omission or addition of the earlier data. Regularly, the new edition simply added to the old, and, as a result, the form of the mass of clay on which these Annals were written changes with the increased length of the document, the earlier being true cylinders, while the latter are prisms.[3] At the same time that the narrative of military events was lengthened, the account of the building operations followed suit. A serious defect is the fact that these documents are dated, not by years, but by campaigns, with the result that there are serious questions in chronology. The increase in the number of our editions, however, has solved many of these, as the date of the campaign

[1]The only fairly complete collection of sources for the reign is still Smith-Sayce, *History of Sennacherib*, 1878, though nearly all the data needed for a study of the Annals are given by Bezold, KB. II. 80ff. Extracts, Rogers, 340ff. Cf. also Olmstead, *Western Asia in the reign of Sennacherib*, Proceedings of Amer. Historical Assn., 1909, 94ff.
[2]Maspero, *Histoire*, III. 273 n. 1.
[3]King, *Cuneiform Texts*, XXVI. 7f.

can now usually be fixed by observing in which dated document it last occurs.

Of the more than twenty five more or less complete documents, the first is the so called Bellino Cylinder which dates from October, 702. The fact that it has been studied separately has tended to prevent the realization that it is actually only a recension. As a first edition, it is a trifle fuller, but surprisingly little.[1] Next comes Cylinder B, now represented by six complete and seven fragmentary cylinders. It includes campaign three and is dated in May, 700.[2] Cylinder C dates from 697 and contains the fourth expedition.[3] The mutilated date of Cylinder D may be either 697 or 695, but as it has one campaign more than Cylinder C of 697, we should probably date it to the latter year.[4] From this recension seems to have been derived the display inscription recently discovered on Mt. Nipur, which was inscribed at the end of campaign five.[5]

Somewhat different from these is the newest Sennacherib inscription,[6] which marks the transition from the shorter to the longer cylinders.[7] After the narrative of the fifth campaign, two others are given, and dated, not by the number of campaign as in the documents of the regular series, but by the eponyms, so that here we have actual chronology. The two campaigns took place in 698 and 695 respectively, the inscription itself being dated in 694. That they are not dated by the campaigns of the

[1]K. 1680. Grotefend, *Abh. Göttingen, Gesell.* 1850. L. 63f. Smith-Sayce, 1f., 24ff., cf. 43ff. Oppert, *Exped.* I. 297ff.; Menant, 225ff.; Talbot, JRAS. XVIII. 76ff.; *Trans. Roy. Soc. Lit.*, VIII, 369ff.; RP¹, I. 23ff. It is the Bl. of Bezold.

[2]Smith-Sayce, 30, 70f., cf. 24, 43, 53; Evetts, ZA. III. 311ff.; for list of tablets, cf. Bezold, *l. c.*

[3]K. 1674; Smith-Sayce, 14, 76, cf. 30, 43, 53, 73, 78. The A 2 of Bezold.

[4]BM. 22,508; K. 1675; Smith-Sayce, 24, 30, 43, 53, 73, 79; King, *Cuneiform Texts*, XXVI. 38, cf. p. 10, n. 2. The A 8 of Bezold.

[5]Inscription at Hasanah (Hassan Agha?) King, PSBA. XXXIV. 66ff.

[6]BM. 103,000; King, *Cuneiform Texts, XXVI;* cf. Pinches, JRAS. 1910, 387ff.

[7]King, *op. cit.*, 9.

king and that they are not given in the later editions is perhaps due to the fact that the king did not conduct them in person.[1] The occasion for this new edition is not to be found, however, in these petty frontier wars, but in the completion of the new palace, in the increase in the size of the city of Nineveh, in the building of a park, and in the installation of a water supply, as these take up nearly a half of the inscription. The recovery of this document has also enabled us to place in the same group two other fragments, now recognized as duplicates.[2]

At about the same time must be placed the various inscriptions on the bulls which were intended to decorate this new palace. One contains only five expeditions,[3] the other has a brief sketch of the sixth,[4] but both have references to the enthronement of the crown prince Ashur nadin shum in Babylon.[5] Still another gives a very full account of the sixth expedition, but there is no mention of Ashur nadin shum.[6] This dates very closely the inscriptions of the period. The new inscription was written in August of 694. At this time as well as when the inscription was placed on Bull II, the news of the sixth expedition, that across the Persian Gulf to Nagitu, had not yet come in. When this arrived, a brief account was hastily compiled and added to Bull III. But before a fuller narrative could be prepared, news came of the capture of Ashur nadin shum, which took place, as we know, soon after the Nagitu expedition, seemingly in the beginning of November.[7] The inscription on Bull IV

[1] King, *op. cit.*, p. 10.
[2] BM. 102, 996, King, *Cuneiform Texts*, XXVI. 38; cf. p. 15, n. 1; K. 4492, ibid. 39, not a reference to Tarbisi, as Meissner-Rost, *Bauinschriften*, 94f.; as is shown by King, p. 18 n. 1.
[3] Bull 2, Smith-Sayce, 3, 24, 30f., 43, 51f., 53, 67f., 73, 78f., 86. L. 60ff. (Bull 1 occurs only Smith-Sayce, 3.)
[4] Bull 3, Smith-Sayce, *l. c.*, and also 88f.
[5] Smith-Sayce, 30f.
[6] Bull 4, Smith-Sayce, 3f., 24, 32ff., 43, 51, 53, 65ff.; 73, 77ff., 89ff.; A. Paterson, *Palace of Sinacherib*, 5f.; III R. 12f.; L. 38ff.
[7] Bab. Chron. II. 36ff.; for *kat Tashriti* in line 40, cf. Delitzsch, *Chronik, ad loc.*

accordingly had an elaborate narrative of the Nagitu expedition, but all mention of the captured prince was cut out.

The last in the series of Annals editions is the Taylor Prism of 690, generally taken as the standard inscription of the reign, and substantially the same text is found on seven other prisms.[1] As has already been made evident, this is of no value for the earlier parts of the reign, since for that we have much better data, but it ranks well up in its class as comparatively little has been omitted or changed. Slightly earlier than the Taylor Cylinder is the Memorial or Nebi Yunus inscription, now at Constantinople, which ends about where the other does. Here and there, it has the same language as the Annals group, but these coincidences are so rare that we must assume that they are due only to the use of well known formulae. In general, it is an abridgement of earlier records, though a few new facts are found. But for the second half of the sixth expedition, the revolt of Babylon, it is our best source. Not only is it fuller than the Taylor prism, it gives a quite different account in which it is not the king but his generals who are the victors. Yet curiously enough, in the seventh expedition the Taylor cylinder is fuller and better.[2]

Here too we may discuss the Bavian inscription, the display inscriptions cut in the rock where began the irrigation works constructed to carry water to the capital. In their historical portions, they parallel the last campaign of the Taylor Prism, though

---

[1] BM. 91,032, often given in photograph, especially in the *"Bible Helps."* A good photograph, Rogers, 543; *Hist.* op. 353. I R. 37ff; Smith-Sayce, *passim;* Delitzsch, *Lesestücke*[4], 54ff.; Abel-Winckler, 17ff. Hörnung, *Das Sechsseitige Prisma des Sanherib*, 1878; Bezold, KB. II. 80ff., with numbers of the duplicates; Oppert, *Les Ins. Assyr. des Sargonides*, 41ff.; Menant, 214ff.; Talbot, RP[1], I. 33ff.; Rogers, RP[2], VI. 80ff.; Harper, 68ff. Here also seem to belong the fragments 79-7-8, 305; K. 1665; 1651; S. 1026, as their text inclines toward that of the Taylor Prism.

[2] I R. 43; A. Paterson, *Palace of Sinacherib*, 3; Smith-Sayce, 7f., 39f., 68f., 86f., 102ff., 111ff., 127ff.; Bezold, KB. II. 118f.; cf. King, *Cuneiform Texts*, XXVI. p. 10 n. 1. Seen at Constantinople in 1907-1908.

in such different fashion that they may be considered separate sources. They then add the final capture and destruction of Babylon, of which they are the only Assyrian authority.[1] Here too may be mentioned the two fragments from the later part of the reign, on which is based a later expedition of Sennacherib against Palestine,[2] as well as a tablet which seems to be a draft of an inscription to be set up in Kirbit in commemoration of the flight of Merodach Baladan.[3]

To complete our study of the sources for the reign, the more specifically building inscriptions may be noted.[4] The greater part of what we know concerning the building operations of the reign comes from the documents already discussed. Of the specifically building inscriptions, perhaps the most important is the New Year's House inscription from Ashur,[5] and the excavations there have also given a good number of display inscriptions on slabs[6] and on bricks,[7] as well as some building prisms.[8]

Esarhaddon (686-668),[9] like the others of his dynasty, prepared elaborate Annals.[10] It is a poetic justice rarely found in history that the man who so ruthlessly destroyed the Annals of

[1] III R. 14; Pognon, *L'inscription de Bavian*, 1879; Smith-Sayce, 129ff.; 157; King, *Tukulti Ninib*, 114ff. Menant, *Nineve et l'Assyrie*, 234ff.; Pinches, RP¹, IX. 21ff.; Bezold, KB. II. 116ff. The order of date is B, C, A, D, Meissner-Rost, *Bauinschriften*, 67. Squeezes were secured by the Cornell Expedition.

[2] Smith-Sayce, 137f.; the later fragment, Scheil, OLZ. VII. 69f.; Ungnad, *Vorderas. Denkmäler*, I. 73ff.; in Gressmann, I. 121; Rogers, 345f.

[3] III R. 4, 4; Strong, JRAS. XXIII. 148ff.

[4] Meissner-Rost, *Bauinschriften Sanheribs*, 1893.

[5] MDOG. 33, 14.

[6] KTA. 43ff., 73f.; MDOG. 21, 13ff.; 22, 17ff.; 26, 27ff.; 43, 31; 44, 29.

[7] I. R. 7, VIII. H; Bezold, KB. 114f.; KTA. 46-49; 72; MDOG. 20, 24; 21, 12ff.; 22, 15; 25, 36f.

[8] MDOG. 21, 37; 25, 22f.; 47, 39.

[9] Inscriptions of the reign collected by Budge, *History of Esarhaddon*, 1880.

[10] First reference, G. Smith, TSBA. III. 457. Boscawen, *ibid.* IV. 84ff.; III R. 35, 4; Budge, 114ff.; Rogers, *Haverford Studies*, II. Winckler, *Untersuch z. altor. Gesch.*, 97f.; Winckler, *Textbuch*, 52ff.; Ung-

Tiglath Pileser IV is today known to us by still smaller fragments of his own. Aside from five mutilated lines from the ninth expedition, only a part of the first expedition against Egypt has survived and that in a very incomplete manner. We are accordingly dependent for our knowledge of the reign on the display inscriptions, with all their possibilities for error, and only the Babylonian Chronicle gives a little help toward fixing the relative order of events.

The greater part of the history of the reign must be secured from the three most important cylinders. A and C are complete and are practically identical.[1] B is broken and was originally considerably fuller, but seems to be from the same general series.[2] The date of all three is probably 673.[3] In comparing the texts of A-C and B, we note that in the first part, there seem to be no important differences, save that B adds an account of the accession. In the broken part before this, B must have given the introduction and the murder of Sennacherib. Computation of the minimum in each column of B, based on the amount actually preserved in A and C, will give us some idea of what has been lost. Column II of B must have been devoted in part to the final defeat of the rebels and in part to the introduction to the

---

nad, I. 123;. Rogers, 357ff. Cf. also G. Smith, *Disc.* 311ff.; Delattre, *L'Asie*, 149; Olmstead, *Bull. Amer. Geog. Soc.*, XLIV. 1912, 434.

[1] 48-10-31, 2; L. 20ff.; I R. 45ff.; Abel-Winckler, 22ff.; Budge, 32ff.; Harper, *Hebraica*, III. 177ff.; IV. 99ff. Abel, KB. II. 124ff.; Oppert, *Ins. des Sargonides*, 53ff.; Talbot, *Jour. Sacr. Lit.*, IX. 68ff.; *Trans. Roy. Soc. Lit.*, VII. 551ff.; RP¹, III 109ff.; Menant, 241ff.; Harper, 81ff. C was used by R. for restoring A. Text, Harper, *Hebraica*, IV. 18ff., with the parallels 80-7-19, 15, and K. 1679. Also King, *Supplement*, 108f.

[2] 48-11-4, 315; III R. 15f.; Budge, 20ff.; 97ff.; Harper, *Hebraica*, III. 177ff.; IV. 146ff.; Abel-Winckler, 25f. Winckler, KB, II. 140ff. Harper, 80f.; Menant, 248ff.; Talbot, RP¹, III. 102ff.; *North Brit. Rev.*, 1870, quoted Harper, *Hebr. l. c.*

[3] C is dated in the month Abu, cf. Harper, *Hebr.* IV. 24; B, according to Budge, *ad loc.*, has Abu of the year 673, but Winckler, *l. c.*, omits the month. If the month is to be retained, the identity of month points to identity of year, and there is nothing in B to prevent this conjecture. A is from Nebi Yunus, B from Koyunjik.

long narrative concerning Nabu zer lishir. As at least four lines were devoted to this introduction in the usually much shorter D, it must have been fairly long in B. Why A omitted all this is a question. That these two events are the first in the reign is made clear by the Babylonian Chronicle, so that thus far the chronological order has been followed. The next event in B and the first in A is the story of the Sidon troubles, and again the Chronicle shows it to be in chronological order. Since A has no less than 49 lines to deal with the events in the lost beginning of column III, it is clear that the much fuller B has here lost much. In the gap in Column IV, we are to place the Aduma narrative and the traces where we can begin to read show that they are in the conclusion of the Median troubles.[1] For the lost part of the fifth column, we must count the Iadi and Gambulu expeditions, and a part of the building narrative. About the same building account as in A must be placed at the commencement of column VI. The irregularity in the minimum numbers for the different columns, on the basis of A, shows that B had in some cases much longer accounts than in others, and this is confirmed where B gives a complete list of Arabian and of Syrian kings while A does not. These minimum numbers also indicate that but about one-fourth of B has been preserved. However, the over lapping gives us some reason to hope that nearly all its facts have been preserved in the one or the other edition.

We have already seen that strict chronology is followed by B, strange to relate, in the order, punishment of the assassins, 681, Babylon, 680, and Sidon, 677. Then A gives the Kundu troubles which, according to the Chronicle, follow in 676, and Arzani and the brook of Egypt, which fit well enough with the Egyptian expedition given under 675. These are the only sections we can date chronologically, and the order is chronologically correct. But whether we can assume this for all the events mentioned may be doubted in the light of the disagreement

[1] *Shepashun* of B. is the *shepushshun* of A. IV. 36, and the *elishun ukin* is virtually the same as *ukin sirushun*.

between A and B in their order. In placing the Arabs before Bazu, or the Babylonian Nabu zer lishir before Bit Dakkuri, A is clearly attempting a more geographical order. We shall then use B as our main source whenever preserved, supplemented by A when the former is missing, but we must not forget that all are simply display inscriptions.

Another display inscription of the same type we shall call D. It is close to B as is shown in the story of Nabu zer lishir, is seemingly briefer than that document, but is certainly fuller than A, and is independent of both. The order of events is Babylon, Egypt, Hubushna. As D omits Sidon and the Cilician cities, found in one of the others and proved to the period by the Babylonian Chronicle, it is clear that we have here only extracts, even though the events narrated are given more fully than in A.[1] Still another document of similar character may be called E. As it mentions the Uabu rebellion which is not in A., it should date after 673, and its order, Chaldaeans, Gambulu, Egypt, Arabs, Sidon, Asia Minor, is not chronological but geographical. It has some striking variants in the proper names, for example, we have here Musur, universally recognized as meaning Egypt, where A has Musri, and thus we have exact proof that Musri does equal Egypt, the advocates of the Musri theory, if any still survive, to the contrary notwithstanding.[2] It is also longer than A. in the River of Egypt section, and than B in the Elam account. As a late document, it is of value only for the Uabu affair.[3] We may also note here another prism fragment[4] and a slab with a brief account of many campaigns. The first, that against Bazu, we know dates to 676. The others, to Uruk, to Buesh king of an unknown land, Akku, and the king of Elam, are of doubtful date, but are almost certainly later.[5]

[1] K. 2671; Winckler, ZA. II. 299ff.; AOF. I. 522.
[2] Cf. Olmstead, *Sargon*, 56ff.
[3] Winckler, ZA. II pl. II; AOF. I. 526ff.
[4] 80-7-19, 15; Winckler, *Untersuch. z. altor. Gesch.*, 98. Cf. King, *Supplement*, 109.
[5] K. 8544; Winckler, AOF. I. 532.—I have been unable to see Scheil, *Le Prisme S d'Assarhaddon*.

Finally, we must discuss two display inscriptions from the very end of the reign, whose importance is in no small degree due to the locality in which they were found. One is the famous stele discovered amid the ruins of the North Syrian town of Sinjirli. It dates after the capture of Memphis, 671, and seems to have been composed on the spot, as it shows no relationship to other inscriptions.[1] The same is probably true of the equally famous rock cut inscription at the Dog River (Nahr el Kelb), north of Berut. Though the oldest Assyrian inscription to have a cast taken, it seems never to have been published. It is rapidly disappearing, as the fact that it was cut through a very thin layer of hard rock has caused much flaking. Esarhaddon is called King of Babylon and King of Musur and Kusi, Egypt and Ethiopia, and the expedition against Tarqu, which ended with the capture and sack of Memphis, is given. Thus it agrees with the Sinjirli inscription and may well date from the same year.[2]

We have a considerable number of building inscriptions, but there are few source problems in connection with them.[3] Perhaps the most important is the prism which tells so much in regard to the earliest days of Assyria.[4] Another important document is the Black Stone, a four sided prism with archaistic writing. It was found at Nineveh, though it deals with the rebuilding of Babylon, and seems to date from the first year.[5] Two

[1] Photograph and text, Schrader, in Luschan, *Ausgrabungen in Sendschirli*, I. 11ff., and pl., cf. Rogers, 551; *Hist*, op. 399; Paterson, *Sculptures*, 103. Harper, 90ff. I have been able to consult squeezes in the library of Cornell University.
[2] Translation, G. Smith, *Eponym Canon*, 167ff. The text, so far as I know, has never been published, even in connection with the elaborate study of the Nahr el Kelb sculptures by Boscawen, TSBA. VII. 345. I have been able to use the squeeze taken in 1904 in connection with Messrs. Charles and Wrench, but much less can now be seen than what Smith evidently found on the cast. Cast, Bonomi, *Trans. Roy. Soc. Lit.*, III. 105; *Nineveh and its Palaces*, 5f. 86. 142ff., 367.
[3] Collected in Meissner-Rost, *Beitr. z. Assyr.*, III. 189ff; Thureau-Dangin, *Rev. Assyr.* XI. 96ff.
[4] KTA. 51; MDOG. 25, 33.
[5] I R. 49; Winckler, KB. II. 120ff.; Meissner-Rost, 218ff. Oppert,

others date after 675 as the one on a stone slab from the south west palace at Kalhu states that he took captive the king of Meluh,[1] and the other stone tablet gives him Egyptian titles,[2] so that they must be placed after the capture of that country. We may also mention in conclusion the one which gives the restoration of the Ishtar temple at Uruk[3] and the various ones found at Ashur by the German excavators.[4]

Exped., I. 180 f.; Menant, 248; *Babylone et Chaldée*, 167f.; Harper, 88f. King, *Supplement*, 38, dates from Aru of accession year.

[1] L. 19a. Winckler, KB. II. 150f. Oppert, *Exped.*, I. 324; Menant, 240.

[2] I R. 48, 5; Winckler, KB. II. 150f.; Meissner-Rost, 204ff.; Menant, 249.

[3] 81-6-7, 209; Winckler, KB, II. 120 n. 1; Barton, *Proc. Amer. Or. Soc.*, 1891, cxxx.

[4] KTA. 51-55; 75; MDOG. 20, 26ff.; 22, 12f.; 25, 33, 65; 26, 20f.; 26, 41ff.; 28, 13, 49, 10f. Weissbach, in Koldewey, *Die Tempel von Babylon*, 71.

CHAPTER VII

ASHUR BANI APAL AND ASSYRIAN EDITING

The reign of Ashur bani apal (668-626), stands preeminent for the mass of material available, and this has twice been collected.[1] Yet in spite of all this, the greater number of the inscriptions for the reign are not before us in adequate form, and there are problems which only a renewed study of the originals can solve.

Once again we have the usual Annals as our main source. Earlier scholars have in general satisfied themselves with the publication and study of the latest edition, sometimes supplemented by more or less full extracts from the others. There are reigns, such as that of Sennacherib, where such procedure results in comparatively little distortion of the history. But in no reign is the distortion of the earlier statements more serious, indeed one can hardly recognize the earlier documents in their later and "corrected" form. Accordingly, in no reign is it more imperative that we should disentangle the various sources and give the proper value to each. When we have discovered which document is our earliest and most authentic source for any given event, we have already solved some of the most stubborn problems in the history of the reign. The various conflicting accounts of the Egyptian campaigns, for example, have caused much trouble, but if we recognize that each is a step in the movement toward increasing the credit the king should receive for them, and trust for our history only the first in date, we have at last placed the history of the reign on a firm basis.

Our very earliest document furnishes a beautiful illustration of this principle. It is a detailed narrative of the unimpor-

[1] G. Smith, *History of Assurbanipal*, 1871; S. A. Smith, *Keilschrifttexte Asurbanipals*, 1887ff.

tant Kirbit expedition, which is ascribed to the governor Nur ekalli umu. Cylinder E gives a briefer account and Cylinder F one still shorter. Both vaguely ascribe it to the "governors" but do not attempt to claim it for the king. It remained for Cylinder B, a score of years later, to take the final step, and to inform us that the king in person conducted the expedition. Further, the formal conclusion, which immediately follows the Kirbit expedition in our earliest document, shows that this event, unimportant as it was, was the only one which could be claimed for the "beginning of the reign." This campaign is further fixed by the Babylonian Chronicle to the accession year. Yet later cylinders can place before it no less than two expeditions against Egypt and one against Tyre! Our earliest document alone would be enough to prove that these had been taken over from the reign of his father, even did we not have some of this verified by that father himself.[1]

Next in date and therefore in value we are probably to place Cylinder E, a decagon fragment, which contains a somewhat less full account of the Kirbit campaign, and a picturesque narrative of the opening of diplomatic relations with Lydia. Before these events, it placed an account of the Egyptian expedition. Although only a portion is preserved, it is sufficient to show that the "first Egyptian expedition" at least was credited to his father.[2]

A third account, which we may call F, gave credit for the earlier half of the Egyptian campaigns to his father and for the latter half to his own lieutenants. The references to Tabal and Arvad indicate that some time had elapsed in which memorable events in his own reign could have taken place, and this is confirmed by the much more developed form of the Lydian narrative, with its dream from Ashur to Gyges, and its order for servitude. That this account is of value as over against the later ones has been recognized,[3] but we should not forget that it al-

[1] K. 2846; Winckler, AOF. I. 474ff.
[2] G. Smith, 34f., 76f., 82f.; K. 3083 is identical for a line each with Cyl. E and F.
[3] Tiele, *Gesch.* 372.

ready represents a developed form of the tradition.[1] Somewhat later would seem to be the account we may call G. Here the Egyptian wars are still counted as one expedition, but a second has been stolen for Ashur bani apal by taking over that campaign of his father against Baal of Tyre which is given in the Sinjirli inscription.[2]

With Cylinder B, we reach the first of what is practically a new series, so greatly has the older narrative been "corrected" in these later documents. Both the Egyptian wars have now been definitely assigned to the king, and the making of two expeditions into Egypt has pushed the one against Baal of Tyre up to the position of third. The octagon B dates from the midst of the revolt of Shamash shum ukin and is a most highly "corrected" document.[3]

The story of the Shamash shum ukin revolt is continued by Cylinder C, a decagon, whose form points to the fact that it is a fuller edition. In general, its text holds an intermediate position between A and B, the lists of Syrian and Cypriote kings, which are copied verbatim from the Cylinder B of Esarhaddon,[4] being found only in it.[5] With C should in all probability be listed two decagons one of which is called Cylinder D.[6] Then comes a document which we may call H, with several duplicates, and as the Ummanaldas episode is dealt with in fuller form than in A,

[1] K. 2675; III R. 28f.; G. Smith, 36ff., 56ff., 73ff., 80ff.; cf. 319 and S. A. Smith, II. 12ff., for ending giving erection of moon temple at Harran, a proof that we have the conclusion and so can date approximately; Winckler, *Untersuch. z. altor. Gesch.*, 102ff.; Jensen, KB. II. 236ff. A fragmentary stone duplicate from Babylon, Delitzsch, MDOG., XVII 2 n.*

[2] K. 3402; G. Smith, 78.

[3] G. Smith, *passim;* Jensen, KB. II. 240ff.; Menant, 278ff.; for the duplicate K. 1729 from which most of the B text is taken, cf. Johns, PSBA. XXVII. 97.

[4] V. 13ff.

[5] Rm. 3; G. Smith, 30ff., 178ff., cf. 15, 52, 151, 319; S. A. Smith, II. 25ff.; Menant, 277f. Jensen, KB. II. 238ff., 266ff.

[6] G. Smith, 317f. K. 1794; III. R. 27a; S. A. Smith, II. 18, cf. G. Smith, 319.

it probably dates earlier.[1] For the Tamaritu events, we have a group of tablets of unknown connections.[2]

All the documents thus far considered are fuller and more accurate in dealing with the events they narrate than is the group which has so long been considered the standard. The first known was Cylinder A, a decagon, whose lines divide the document into thirteen parts. It is dated the first of Nisan (March) in the eponymy of Shamash dananni, probably 644.[3] Earlier scholars made this the basis of study, but it has since been supplanted by the so called Rassam cylinder, a slightly better preserved copy, found in the north palace of Nineveh, and dated in Aru (May) of the same year.[4] Still a third is dated in Ululu (September) of this year.[5]

That this document is by no means impeccable has long been recognized. Already George Smith had written "The contempt of chronology in the Assyrian records is well shown by the fact that in Cylinder A, the account of the revolt of Psammitichus is given under the third expedition, while the general account of the rebellion of [Shamash shum ukin] is given under the sixth expedition, the affair of Nebobelzikri under the eighth expedition, and the Arabian and Syrian events in connection are given under the ninth expedition."[6] If this severe criticism is not justified by a study of the Assyrian sources as a whole, the reference to Cylinder A may well begin our consideration of the shortcomings of that group. The Karbit and Urtaki episodes

---

[1] K. 2656; G. Smith, 215ff. Are the duplicates mentioned here to be found in K. 2833 and K. 3085, G. Smith, 205?

[2] K. 1364; 3062; 2664; 3101; 2631/; G. Smith, 243ff.—Where we are to place the cylinder Rm. 281, dealing with Urtaki's reign, Winckler, AOF. I. 478 n. 2, cannot be told until it is published.

[3] G. Smith, passim, III R. 17ff. RP¹, IX 37ff.; Menant, 253ff.

[4] BM. 91,026; Rm. 1; Photograph, Rogers, 555; Hist. op. 444. V. R. 1-10; Abel-Winckler, 26ff.; Winckler, Sammlung, III; S. A. Smith, I. Jensen, KB. II. 152ff. J. M. P. Smith, in Harper, 94ff.; Lau & Langdon, Annals of Ashurbanapal, 1903.

[5] G. Smith, 316.

[6] Ibid. 202 n.*

are entirely omitted. The omission of Karbit has dropped the Manna from the fifth to fourth and the omission of the latter has made the Teumman campaign the fifth instead of the seventh as in B, while the Gambulu expedition is also listed in the fifth though B makes it the eighth! The death of Gyges is added immediately after the other Lydian narrative, without a hint that years had intervened. The elaborate account of Teumman given by B has been cut decidedly and the interesting Ishtar dream is entirely omitted.

The same is true of the Gambulu narrative. While B and C have the data as to the Elamite side of the revolt of Shamash shum ukin, the introduction and conclusion as well as many new details are found only in A. It is curious to find here, for the first time, the greater part of the long list of conquered Egyptian kings, written down when Egypt was forever freed from Assyrian rule. That Cylinder B was not its immediate source is shown by the fact that in the first Egyptian expedition it gives the pardon of Necho, which is not in B, but is found in the earlier F.

Although this document has regularly been presented as the base text, largely because it gives a view of the greater part of the reign, enough should have been said in the preceding paragraph to prove how unworthy of the honor it is. Of all the cases where such procedure has caused damage, this is the worst. For the years from which we have no other data, we must use it, and we may hope that, as this period was nearer the time of its editors, its information may here be of more value. But we should recognize once and for all that the other portions are worthless and worse than worthless, save as they indicate the "corrections" to the actual history thought necessary by the royal scribes.

Later than this in date, in all probability, is the document we may call I. To be sure, the Arabian expedition already occurs in B, but I has also sections which appear only in A, and which therefore probably date later. The one indication that points to its being later than A is the fact that, while A ascribes these actions to his generals, our document speaks of them in the first person.[1] Still later are the Beltis[2] and Nabu inscriptions,[3] though as these are merely display inscriptions, the date matters little. Here too belongs J in spite of its references to the accession.[4] And to this very late period, when the empire was falling to pieces, is to be placed the hymn to Marduk which speaks of Tugdami the Cilician.[5]

We have already crossed the boundary which divides the really historical narratives from those which are merely sources. Among the latter, and of the more value as they open to us the sculptures, are the frequent notes inscribed over them,[6] while a number of tablets give much new historical information from the similar notes which the scribe was to thus incise.[7] The Ishtar prayer is a historic document of the first class, the more so as its author never dreamed that some day it might be used to prove that the king was not accustomed, as his annals declare, to go forth at the head of his armies, that he was, in fact, destitute of even common bravery.[8]

For the period after the reign of Ashur bani apal, we have only the scantiest data. The fall of the empire was imminent and there were no glories for the scribe to chronicle. Some bricks from the south east palace at Kalhu,[9] some from Nippur,[10] and some boundary inscriptions[11] are all that we have from Ashur

[1] K. 2802; G. Smith, 290ff.

[2] II R. 66; G. Smith 303ff.; S. A. Smith, II. 10ff.; cf. I. 112; Jensen, KB. II. 264ff.; Menant, 291ff.

[3] S. A. Smith, I. 112ff.; III. 128ff.; Strong, RA. II. 20ff.

[4] K. 2867; S. A. Smith, II. 1ff.; cf. Olmstead, *Bull. Amer. Geog. Soc.*, XLIV. 434.—The various British Museum fragments, cited in King, *Supplement*, seem to be of no special importance for this study as they are duplicates with few variants.

[5] S. A. Strong, JA. 1893, 1. 368ff.

[6] Scattered through the work of G. Smith, cf. also Menant, 287ff.

[7] K. 2674; III R. 37; G. Smith, 140ff.; S. A. Smith, III. 1ff. K. 4457; G. Smith, 191ff. K. 3096; G. Smith, 295ff.

[8] K. 2652; III R. 16, 4; G. Smith, 139f.; S. A. Smith, III. 11ff.; cf. Jensen, KB. II. 246ff. Talbot, TSBA. I. 346ff.

[9] I R. 8, 3; Winckler, KB. II. 268f.; Menant, 295.

[10] Hilprecht, ZA. IV. 164; *Explorations*, 310.

[11] K. 6223, 6332; Winckler, AOF. II. 4f; Johns. PSBA. XX. 234.

itil ilani and from Sin shar ishkun only fragments of a cylinder dealing with building.[1] We have no contemporaneous Assyrian sources for the fall of the kingdom, our only certain knowledge being derived from a mutilated letter[2] and from a brief statement of the Babylonian king Nabu naid a generation later.[3]

[1]K. 1662 and dupl. I R. 8, 6; Schrader, *SB. Berl. Gesell.* 1880, 1ff.; Winckler, *Rev. Assyr.* II. 66ff.; KB. II. 270ff.; MDOG. XXXVIII. 28.
[2]BM. 51082; Thompson, *Late Babylonian Letters* 248.
[3]Messerschmidt, *Mitth. Vorderas. Gesell.*, 1896. I.

CHAPTER VIII

THE BABYLONIAN CHRONICLE AND BEROSSUS

This concludes our detailed study of the "histories" of the reigns which were set forth with the official sanction. Before summing up our conclusions as to their general character, it will be well to devote a moment to the consideration of certain other sources for the Assyrian period. Many minor inscriptions have been passed by without notice, and a mere mention of the mass of business documents, letters, and appeals to the sun god will here be sufficient, though in a detailed history their help will be constantly invoked to fill in the sketch secured by the study of the official documents, and not infrequently to correct them. Of foreign sources, those of the Hebrews furnish too complicated a problem for study in this place,[1] and the scanty documents of the other peoples who used the cuneiform characters hardly furnish source problems.

Even the Babylonians have furnished us with hardly a text which demands source study. To the end, as is shown so conspicuously in the case of Nebuchadnezzar, scores of long inscriptions could be devoted to the building activities of the ruler while a tiny fragment is all that is found of the Annals. Even his rock cut inscriptions in Syria, those in the Wadi Brissa and at the Nahr el Kelb, are almost exclusively devoted to architectural operations in far away Babylon![2]

Yet if the Babylonians were so deficient in their appreciation of the need of historical annals for the individual reigns, they seem to have been the superiors of the Assyrians when it came to the production of actual histories dealing with long

---

[1]Cf. Olmstead, AJSL. XXX. 1ff.; XXXI. 169ff., for introduction to these new problems.

[2]It may be noted that the Cornell Expedition secured squeezes of both these inscriptions.

periods of time. While the Babylonians have preserved to us numerous lists of kings and two excellent works which we have every reason to call actual histories, the Babylonian Chronicle and the Nabunaid-Cyrus Chronicle, the Assyrians have but the Eponym Lists, the so called Assyrian Chronicle, and the so called Synchronous History. The last has already been discussed, and we have seen how little it deserved the title of a real history, yet it marks the greatest advance the Assyrians made along this line. The Eponym lists are merely lists of the officials who dated each year in rotation, and they seem to have been compiled for practical calendar purposes. The so called Assyrian Chronicle is in reality nothing but a chronological table in three columns, the first with the name of the eponym for the year, the second with his office, and the third with the most important event, generally a campaign, of the year. As a historical source, more can be made out of this dry list than has previously been suspected, and this has been pointed out elsewhere.[1] But, as a contribution to the writing of history, it holds a distinctly low place.

On the other hand, the Babylonian Chronicle is a real, if somewhat crude history. In fact, it can be said without fear of contradiction that it is the best historical production of any cuneiform people. Our present copy is dated in the twenty second year of Darius I of Persia, 500 B. C., but, as it was copied and revised from an earlier exemplar, which could not always be read, its original must be a good bit earlier. Only the first tablet has come down to us, but the mention of the first proves that a second existed. What we have covers the period 745-668, a period of seventy-seven years. The second tablet would cover a period nearer the time of the writer and would naturally deal with the events more in detail, so that a smaller number of years would be given on this tablet. If but two tablets were written, the end of the work would be brought down close to the time when the Assyrian Empire fell (608). It is a tempting conjecture, though nothing more, that it was the fall of Assyria and the in-

[1] Olmstead, *Jour. Amer. Or. Soc.*, XXXIV. 344ff.

terest in the relations between the now dominant Babylonia and its former mistress, excited by this event, which led to the composition of the work. Be that as it may, the author is remarkably fair, with no apparent prejudice for or against any of the nations or persons named. The events chosen are naturally almost exclusively of a military or political nature, but within these limits he seems to have chosen wisely. In general, he confines himself to those events which have an immediate bearing on Babylonian history, but at times, as, for example, in his narration of the Egyptian expeditions, he shows a rather surprising range of interest. If we miss the picturesque language which adds so much to the literary value of the Assyrian royal annals, this can hardly be counted an objection by a generation of historians which has so subordinated the art of historical writing to the scientific discovery of historical facts. In its sobriety of presentation and its coldly impartial statement of fact, it may almost be called modern.[1]

We know the name of our other Babylonian historian, and we also know his date, though unfortunately we do not know his work in its entirety. This was Berossus, the Babylonian priest, who prepared a Babyloniaca which was dedicated to Antiochus I. When we remember that it is this same Antiochus who is the only one of the Seleucidae to furnish us with an inscription in cuneiform and to the honor of one of the old gods,[2] it becomes clear that this work was prepared at the time when fusion of Greek and Babylonian seemed most possible, and with the desire to acquaint the Macedonian conquerors with the deeds of their predecessors in the rule of Babylonia. The book was characteristically Babylonian in that only the last of the three books

---

[1]Photograph, Rogers, 515. C. T. XXXIV 43ff. Abstract, Pinches, PSBA. VI. 198ff. Winckler, ZA. II. 148ff.; Pinches, JRAS. XIX. 655ff. Abel-Winckler, 47f. Duplicates, Bezold, PSBA. 1889, 181; Delitzsch, *Lesestücke*[4], 137ff. Schrader, KB. II. 274ff.; Delitzsch, *Bab. Chronik;* Rogers, 208ff.; Barta, in Harper, 200ff. Sarsowsky, *Keilschriftliches Urkundenbuch*, 49ff.; Mercer, *Extra Biblical Sources*, 65ff.

[2]Best in Weissbach, *Achämeniden Inschriften*, 132ff., cf. xxx for bibliography.

ASSYRIAN HISTORIOGRAPHY 63

into which it was divided, that beginning with the time of Nabonassar, can be considered historical in the strictest sense, and even of this only the merest fragments, abstracts, or traces, have come down to us. And the most important of these fragments have come down through a tradition almost without parallel. Today we must consult a modern Latin translation of an Armenian translation of the lost Greek original of the Chronicle of Eusebius,[1] who borrowed in part from Alexander Polyhistor who borrowed from Berossus direct, in part from Abydenus who apparently borrowed from Juba who borrowed from Alexander Polyhistor and so from Berossus. To make a worse confusion, Eusebius has in some cases not recognized the fact that Abydenus is only a feeble echo of Polyhistor, and has quoted the accounts of each side by side! And this is not the worst. Although his Polyhistor account is in general to be preferred, Eusebius seems to have used a poor manuscript of that author. Furthermore, there is at least one case, that of the name of one of Sennacharib's sons, which can be secured only by assuming a mistake in the Armenian alphabet.

It is in Eusebius that we find our most useful information, some of the facts being very real additions to our knowledge. But Berossus was also used by the early Apollodorus Chronicle, some time after 144 B. C., from which some of his information may have drifted into other chronological writings. Alexander Polyhistor was used by Josephus, and Abydenus by Cyrillus, Syncellus, and the Armenian historian, the pseudo Moses of Chorene. So in these too, or even in others not here named, may lurk stray trifles from the work of Berossus. Perhaps from this, or from a similar source, comes the Babylonian part of the list of Kings known as the Canon of Ptolemy, which begins, as does the Babylonian Chronicle, with the accession of Nabonassar.[2] Though directly of Egyptian origin, as is shown by the system of

[1] A. Schoene, *Eusebii Chronicorum libri duo*, 1866ff.; cf. Rogers, *Parallels*, 347ff.; J. Karst, *Eusebius Werke*, V.

[2] The most convenient edition Wachsmuth, *Einleitung in das Studium der alten Geschichte*, 304ff.; cf. Rogers, 239.

dating, it undoubtedly goes back to a first class Babylonian source, as do the astronomical data in the Almagest of the same author, though here too the Egyptian calendar is used.[1] Summing up, practically all the authentic knowledge that the classical world has of the Assyrians and Babylonians came from Berossus.[2] Herodotus may furnish a bit and something may be secured from the fragments of the Assyriaca of Ctesias, but it is necessary to test each fact from other sources before it can be accepted.

And now what shall we say by way of summing up the Assyrian writing of history? First of all, it was developed from the building inscription and not from the boast of the soldier. That this throws a new light on the Assyrian character must be admitted, though here is not the place to prove that the Assyrian was far more than a mere man of war. All through the development of the Assyrian historiography, the building operations play a large part, and they dominate some even of the so called Annals. But once we have Annals, the other types of inscriptions may generally be disregarded. The Annals inscriptions, then, represent the height of Assyrian historical writing. From the literary point of view, they are often most striking with their bold similes, and that great care was devoted to their production can frequently be proved. But in their utilization, two principles must constantly be kept in mind. One is that the typical annals inscription went through a series of editions, that these later editions not only omitted important facts but "corrected" the earlier recitals for the greater glory of the ruler, real or nominal, and that accordingly only the earliest edition in which an event is narrated should be at all used. Secondly, we should never forget that these are official documents, and that if we can trust them in certain respects the more because they had better opportuni-

---

[1] Cf. Olmstead, *Sargon*, 34f.

[2] Of the literature on Berossus, we may quote here only Müller, *Fragmenta Historicorum Graecorum*, II. 495ff.; and the various articles by Schwartz, on Abydenus, Alexandros 88, and Berossus, in the Pauly-Wissowa *Real-encyclopädie*.

ties for securing the truth, all the greater must be our suspicion that they have concealed the truth when it was not to the advantage of the monarch glorified. Only when we have applied these principles in detail to the various documents can we be sure of our Assyrian history and only then shall we understand the mental processes of the Assyrian historians.

ABBREVIATIONS

Abel-Winckler	L. Abel, H. Winckler, Keilschrifttexte, 1890.
AJSL	American Journal of Semitic Languages.
Amiaud-Scheil	A. Amiaud, V. Scheil, Les inscriptions de Salmanassar II, 1890.
AOF	H. Winckler, Altorientalische Forschungen, 1893ff.
BM	British Museum number; special collections are marked K., S., Rm., DT., or by the year, month, and day, as 81-2-3, 79.
Budge	E. A. W. Budge, History of Esarhaddon, 1880.
Budge-King	E. A. W. Budge, L. W. King, Annals of Kings of Assyria, I. 1902.
G. Smith	G. Smith, History of Assurbanipal, 1871.
Harper	R. F. Harper, Assyrian and Babylonian Literature, 1901.
JA	Journal Asiatique.
JRAS	Journal of the Royal Asiatic Society.
KB	E. Schrader, Keilschriftliche Bibliothek, 1889ff.
KTA	L. Messerschmidt, Keilschrifttexte aus Assur, I. 1911.
L	A. H. Layard, Inscriptions in the Cuneiform Character, 1851.
Le Gac	Y. le Gac, Les inscriptions d'Assur-nasir-apal III, 1907.
MDOG	Mittheilungen der Deutschen Orient Gesellschaft.
Menant	Menant, Annales des rois d'Assyrie, 1874.
NR	A. H. Layard, Nineveh and its Remains, 1851.
OLZ	Orientalistische Literaturzeitung.
PSBA	Proceedings of the Society of Biblical Archaeology.
R	H. C. Rawlinson, Cuneiform Inscriptions of Western Asia, 1861ff.
Rasmussen	N. Rasmussen, Salmanasser den II's Indskriften.
Rogers	R. W. Rogers, Cuneiform Parallels to the Old Testament, 1912.
Rost	P. Rost, Keilschrifttexte Tiglat-Pilesers, 1893.
RP	Records of the Past, Ser. I. 1875ff.; Ser. II. 1889ff.
RT	Recueil de Travaux.
S. A. Smith	S. A. Smith, Keilschrifttexte Asurbanipals, 1887ff.
Smith-Sayce	G. Smith, A. H. Sayce, History of Sennacherib, 1878.
TSBA	Transactions of the Society of Biblical Archaeology.
Ungnad	A. Ungnad, in H. Gressmann, Altorientalische Texte, 1909.
ZA	Zeitschrift für Assyriologie.

www.ingramcontent.com/pod-product-compliance
Lightning Source LLC
Chambersburg PA
CBHW061508040426
42450CB00008B/1530